PLAYS
BASED ON STORIES BY SRI CHINMOY

VOLUME I

Sumangali Morhall

Copyright © 2019 Sumangali Morhall

No portion of this book may be reproduced in any form without express written permission from the publisher.

ISBN: 978-1-911319-99-3

GANAPATI PRESS

CONTENTS

1	SATYAVAMA'S PERFECT HUSBAND	9
2	THE PILGRIMAGE TO SANTIAGO	19
3	MIRABAI	43
4	KRISHNA'S VICTORY	59
5	THE PRINCESS AND THE PIRATE	73
6	THE SEEKER-WRITER	97
7	WE NEED MONEY-POWER TO LIVE ON EARTH	109
8	LAOSEN DOES THE IMPOSSIBLE	123
9	THE GODS GAIN IMMORTALITY	135
10	CONVERSATIONS	149

PREFACE

These rhyming plays began on a Christmas Trip with Sri Chinmoy in China, December 2004. On our winter retreats, as well as meditating with Sri Chinmoy in person, we had the privilege of immersing ourselves in his new creations: songs, prayers, aphorisms, stories and artwork. In the evenings it usually fell to us, his disciples, to entertain one another on stage. Much of the programme consisted of plays based on the Master's stories – some of which are tales retold from Indian folklore, others anecdotes from Sri Chinmoy's own experience, others born of his own creative imagination, and many seemingly from delightful worlds between.

    I rarely involved myself in plays up until then. I was – and still am – terrible at acting. My self-consciousness and inability to handle pressure led to a chaos of forgetfulness on stage. It saddened me not to contribute though, so that year in China I decided to take a risk and play to my strengths. I like to write. I could reliably read something out from paper. I could draw some faces on card, cut out holes for eyes, and tie them back as make-shift masks. The characters would mime, while others – including myself – would read their lines into a microphone off-stage. Hence everyone was hiding, which suited me well. The actors did not need to memorise their lines verbatim, which suited them too.

    I was quite sure it would end in disaster even before it began, but to my surprise there were no accidents, even amongst the short-sighted, and any confusion was only a minor distraction. Sri Chinmoy was attentive, and I dare say even seemed quite pleased, which astonished me no end. So a new tradition began, and has continued beyond the Master's passing, as the Sri Chinmoy Centre meets each year for Christmas Trips.

    As with all his art forms, Sri Chinmoy's stories spring

from a source of meditation, and convey his timeless spiritual teachings. While the Master encouraged us to embellish them in our plays, this is a fine line to tread. I sincerely hope to have kept the essential message in each, and above all encourage the reader to enjoy them in the original.

ACKNOWLEDGEMENTS

All gratitude to Sri Chinmoy for these illumining stories, and for allowing us to interpret them in our own limited and childly way. Deep thanks also to Alo Devi for her keen interest and encouragement over the years. Last but not least, my heartfelt thanks to all the actors for their enthusiasm, imagination and patience – for turning dreams into reality.

NOTES ON READING

While I dabbled in various poetic metres in the first four scripts – tetrameter, pentameter, and rather looser forms in the case of the second – I eventually settled on common metre, traditional in hymns and ballads. Though such verse is usually written in quatrains, I prefer it in rhyming couplets of seven beats (heptameter), as that makes it easier to read in performances. In the first four scripts, emphasis is generally on the second syllable (iambic). In the rest, emphasis is generally on the first syllable (trochaic), but sometimes an extra syllable is sneaked in before the first, rather like a grace note in music. So as not to trip the reader up, these are marked in grey.

In all ten scripts, there have been minor edits to the originals. These little plays are still far from perfect, but I hope they bring some joy.

Sumangali Morhall
York, February 14th 2019

1
SATYAVAMA'S PERFECT HUSBAND

BASED ON THE STORY BY SRI CHINMOY:
SATYAVAMA'S PERFECT HUSBAND [1]

CAST

KRISHNA
SATYAVAMA
SATRAJIT (YADAVA KING, SATYAVAMA'S FATHER)
SATYAVAMA'S MOTHER
A SUITOR

First performed in Xiamen, China
December 11th 2004

PROLOGUE

(Enter Krishna.)

KRISHNA
Of all luminaries, I am the sun,
Of measurements, time, since time was begun.
The glory of glorious, all enterprise,
I am the wisdom of all the wise.

(Exit Krishna.)

SCENE 1

(At the palace, parental home of Satyavama.)

(Enter Satrajit.)

SATRAJIT
My daughter is of the marrying age,
For her it's a rather awkward stage.
She'll only accept one who'll do as she asks.
She'll set him all kinds of impossible tasks!
He must obey her… or risk being killed,
She really is frightfully iron-willed.
Oh God! Here comes my… charming wife,
   (Enter Mother, flustered.)
Hello my ladoo… er… love of my life!

MOTHER
Oh who will marry one so obstinate?
She's now seventeen, it is getting too late!
It's really *your* fault, as you wanted a *boy*!

Will a warrior wife bring any man joy?
Those hours in the sun with a sword or a mace
Have darkened and hardened her delicate face!
She will not wear jewellery, she can't even cook!
Who'll even give her a second look?

SATRAJIT
Don't be so hard on our only child,
It's quite the trend to be wilful and wild.
Still yet we may find her a suitor who dares,
But if we don't find him, so be it, who cares?

(Satrajit opens a newspaper dismissively, but Mother pulls it away.)

MOTHER
An unmarried daughter?! How inauspicious!
The neighbours will think it highly suspicious!
There's one more young man who will possibly cope,
He is our sweet darling's only hope.
Let's meet him in person – that fine army fellow.
At least come and see him and say your hello.

(Enter Suitor, giving a showy marching display.)

SUITOR
I hope she does not have an enquiring mind,
The modest type is so very refined.
She should be attentive, reflective, poetic,
A lady should never be too energetic.
Can she cook aloo gobi without too much spice?
I like al dente pilau rice.
She mustn't wear purple. I hope she's artistic.
And then there's the matter of vital statistics.

FATHER
Excuse us now, we've a few things to do,
And don't call us, thanks, we'll call you!

(Satrajit bundles Suitor firmly off stage. Enter Satyavama, wearing purple, practising sword fighting.)

SATYAVAMA
Oh Father! There you are, where have you been?

SATRAJIT
There was a young man whom we hadn't yet seen.

MOTHER
He's learnèd, charming, well-groomed and polite.

SATYAVAMA
Obedient too? Would he give the green light
To my very slightest fleeting whim?

SATRAJIT
Not quite, no.

SATYAVAMA
Then let's disregard him.

MOTHER *(jumping up and down)*
Oh hell!

SATRAJIT *(shrugging shoulders)*
Oh well.

MOTHER
You are *impossible*, Satyavama,

The only men left are the priest and a farmer!
You will be the death of your poor old mother.

(Mother swoons and is caught by Satrajit.)

SATYAVAMA
Just think about it… there is one other.

(Exit Mother and Satyavama. Door bell rings, Satrajit answers. Enter Krishna.)

SATRAJIT
Come, Krishna! To what do we owe this visit?
(Krishna hands over a jewel in a cloth.)
My long lost Syamantaka diamond is it!?
My preciousss! How did you happen across it?
Some say you stole it, or my brother lost it.

KRISHNA
The latter more like, but it's quite a long story,
And most of it actually is quite gory.
It'll do for a more swashbuckling play,
We haven't got time for it all today.
So now in exchange for your jewel's return,
You may be fairly surprised to learn:
Your daughter is destined to be my wife.

SATRAJIT
Your what?! She'll make you a slave for life!
You'll have to be at her beck and call,
There'll be no room for your own will at all.
Trust me, I've been married for twenty years
To someone who speaks but rarely hears.

(Mother sneaks on stage straining to eavesdrop.)

KRISHNA
It is my fate and it is hers too,
And so there is nothing I'd rather do.

MOTHER *(hysterical)*
Do my ears deceive me? O happiest day!
Call the priest, the florist, photographer! Yay!

(Enter Satyavama. Wedding procession. Krishna and Satyavama sedate and soulful, followed by the hysterical family. Exit family.)

SCENE 2

(At Krishna's palace.)

SATYAVAMA
Now Krishna, sit! Now Krishna, stand!
Now catch the moon for me in one hand!

KRISHNA
I will bring your every heart's desire,
But there is *one* thing that I first require:
I just ask that you look at me
While you make your each new plea.

(Satyavama glances at Krishna.)

SATYAVAMA
I know where you are, now you sit down,
And make me a funny face like a clown.

KRISHNA
All right, agreed, your eyes can see,
But do you really *look* at me?

(Satyavama looks properly while trying to speak.)

SATYAVAMA
Now Krishna…

KRISHNA
Satyavama, what?

SATYAVAMA
Oh… what was it? I completely forgot. *(angrily looks away)*
No! How is this a fair condition?
Now yours is an advantageous position!
If I am to ask while I properly look,
I'll be caught by some invisible hook! *(turns soulful)*
Then I'll be trapped with rapt surprise,
As where there would be human eyes
A storm of galaxies is raging,
Ever changing, never ageing.
For a smile instead I see
A panoramic rhapsody,
And there I lose my tiny will,
Desire's torrent frozen still.
Who are you, Krishna?

KRISHNA
Who am I not?
How has your very heart forgot
The one who knows your every breath,
To love beyond the veil of death?
Who else would follow you that far?

Have you remembered who *you* are?

(Satyavama looks at Krishna in stillness and silence, then mimics Krishna's movements.)

SATYAVAMA
One who is lost in the fields of your joys,
One who needs no more outer toys.
I fight when you fight, I dream what you dream,
I am the life-partner of the Supreme.

2
THE PILGRIMAGE TO SANTIAGO

BASED ON THE STORIES BY SRI CHINMOY:
WISDOM CAME LATE [2]
MONEY CORRUPTS [3]
THE TRAVELLER'S PAYMENT [4]
THE THREE QUESTIONS [5]
THE RICH MAN RENOUNCES THE WORLD [6]

CAST
DUKE
COOK
STABLE BOY
HORSEMAN
PILGRIM
VENDOR
HERMIT
THE VIRGIN MARY
DUCHESS
SON OF DUKE AND DUCHESS
NARRATOR

First performed in Kuantan, Malaysia
December 21ˢᵗ 2005

SCENE 1

(In the kitchen, at the home of the Duke.)

(Enter Cook.)

NARRATOR
Behold the humble kitchen boy, at work but feeling nervous,
Awaits the English nobleman who keeps him in his service.
The volatile but kindly Duke some pity on him took,
At birth abandoned, but with time he's blossomed as a cook.
His spirit stays in bloom despite the household's eccentricity,
In fact the outer turbulence just adds to his felicity.
Hush now, the Duke beneath the stairs will make a rare appearance.
He's heard the boy is leaving home, which prompts his interference.

(Cook busies himself. Enter Duke.)

DUKE
You *what*!? *(Duke leans on stove, Cook jumps)*

COOK
Hot… *hot*! *(Duke jumps)*
…Do I displease you Sire?

DUKE (*angrily*)
Did I raise you from that mire
In which some tawdry ungenerous bint
Spawned and cast you sans care, sans hint
Of mortal wound or even sadness?
Frolicked off with all the madness
Of a hare in spring

Left you sans the meagrest thing
To call your own
Whimpering softly all alone!

COOK
Sire, my very breath today submits to you with gratitude,
But mother had no callousness in granting me my latitude.
She did but die of her own accord, *(matter of factly)*
And father then could scarce afford...

DUKE
Do you displease me? Oh ho ho!
With whom and wither will you go?
And why and howso cruelly wrenched?
When here since hapless birth entrenched...

COOK
I leave alone, Sire, as you found me,
No wall or blanket to surround me.
Boar and ant to be my brothers,
Trees my sisters, clouds my mothers,
Cousin of the night sky...

DUKE
Yes, yes, but prithee why?

COOK
...The heather knoll my hermitage...
Oh...! I am bound for *pilgrimage*!

(Musical interlude. Duke looks around, bemused.)

DUKE
Yes, I see, but prithee why?

We too have ants and trees and sky.
What here offends, what in you ails?
Why has your fancy sprouted sails?
A handsome wage, an ample bed,
The finest cook, so art well fed…

COOK
Perhaps there simply comes a day
For each man, when the soul holds sway.
A new man then would burst to burgeon!
With a vastness merge and
Fly abroad from comforts itchy!
The cosy, of a sudden… twitchy!

DUKE
You've found a girl, oh now I see! *(laughing fondly)*
'Tis no religious mystery.
Stay! Why elope and flee afar?
Come now, this calls for a cigar.

(Cook takes cigar, puzzled, and puts it in his pocket.)

COOK
Sire, be sure my word is true!
Not once a secret held from you!
The soul with loneness I regale,
Not some fawning, limp female!

DUKE
…Then how far your destination?
Whence sans good remuneration
Now usurps thee from my side?
Hemel Hempstead? East Kilbride?

COOK
Four days at least... had I a mule.
To force a beast would be too cruel,
So eight... that is from Puente la Reina
Which is the other side of Spain... er.

DUKE
Then?!

COOK
When?
Oh, Santiago, and the relics of St James!
   (More music. Duke looks around, bemused.)
Via Navarre! Castile! ... and certain other names...

DUKE
You will travel by foot, long day upon day –
It seems you have not yet determined which way –
Befriending the insects, and hunger, and thirst.
Surely the perishing nights will be worst.
You'll dabble in swamps, and scrabble on stones,
All in search of an old pile of *bones*?
You are not even fit to clean a pot!
Nor warm the pan for the foot of my cot!
Though I knew you were simple, some call you dense...
Be gone, unthankful loon! Get thee hence!

   (Exit Duke. Cook shakes head, shrugs, exits.)

SCENE 2

(Outside the Duke's house.)

(Enter Stable Boy, leans against tree.)

NARRATOR
Behold the simple stable lad is musing by a tree,
The cook's mate through thick and thin, since they both were three.
Watch him though – you'll see in him the makings of a rogue,
He wears his mischief jauntily as if it were in vogue.

(Enter Cook, in a rush.)

STABLE BOY *(to audience)*
He scuttles with a beetle's haste.

COOK
Chum! Come! No time to waste! *(breathless)*

(Stable Boy fans him and props him against the tree.)

COOK
I have along this little life a little fortune massed,
But now a calling to a rather broader venture hast
Befallen me, I know not how
Only that I must leave now!
I take with me a little share and trust to you the surplus.
To anyone on pilgrimage such cargo would be worthless.

STABLE BOY *(listening to the ground)*
Thou worriest thy mother's bones – I feel it in the earth.
Aye me, a subtle madness now has got thee by the girth.

COOK
Spare me the professor's tone now brother, I beseech thee.
Mine's a subtle education – only pilgrim roads can teach me.
   (hands over money)
I've been sliced, scalded, diced, scolded, sautéed in its earning.
There's only you have earned my faith to guard 'til my returning.

STABLE BOY *(gravely nodding)*
Hail pilgrim, "who would valiant be 'gainst all disaster,
Let him in constancy follow the Master." [7]
Amen. Now I'll write you a receipt.

COOK
The object of a friendship now you purpose to defeat.
No, no! Our brothers' love is needless of certificate.
Would my trust not far transcend a simple moral etiquette?

STABLE BOY
I salute your rectitude, and say again, Amen. *(listening)*
The winds invite your solitude... well hurry to them then!

COOK
Has anywhere in Christendom seen such a friend as you?
   (exiting)
Fret not for me, nor pine for me! Adieu...! Adieu...! Adieu...!

STABLE BOY *(to the audience, counting money)*
Here's fuel for my winter... and the finest coat of wool,
Just watch the maids return my wink now that my coffer's full.

(Exeunt.)

SCENE 3

(On a country road.)

(Enter Cook.)

NARRATOR
One hour has passed, the pilgrim's feet have started their complaining.
He's fearful of the road ahead – you see his spirit waning?
A shower of rain is gathering and trickles down his back,
He's weighed down by his homesick pangs and hefty sodden pack.

(Enter Horseman.)

HORSEMAN
How now lad, what's this? Art thou escaping from the law?
Or signing up for navy ships in case we have a war?
Where e'er you're bound, I'm doubting now that those two feet'll take you.
You need legs in all four corners or these roads'll break you.

COOK
Good sir, my flight is surely not belligerent or criminal,
This journey made on these two legs is pure, and purely seminal.
I am pilgrim, sir – I'll not despair if I am weary.
What brighter way to start the day than with a sound so cheery
As your send-off sir, but tarry not, the road does beckon!
   (Horseman goes to leave, but Cook calls him back)
Could those four legs... bear a little more? What do you reckon?
This pack would be as matchstick to a steed so lithe and strong.

This night I am for Croydon bound, and still the way is long.
Would it be a bother to secrete it for me there?
I'll recover it at nightfall... I could pay a little fare?

HORSEMAN
No bother, and no fare. I'll be at Croydon in a trice.
Pass it to the saddle lest I think about it twice.

COOK
Oh, may the chuckling sun's delight abound throughout your day!
(Horseman looks up at rain)
A truly noble soul assists a pilgrim on his way.

HORSEMAN *(darkly, starts to leave)*
You'll find it in the Dark Barn at old Albany Farm.

COOK *(to audience)*
There's money there and much besides... if it should come to harm...
(to Horseman:)
Sir, please wait! My conscience bites me like a bitter snake.
The burden's mine, I'll bear it, here's a pilgrim's pride at stake!

HORSEMAN
Back and forth, come and go,
Up and down, to and fro.
Methinks he has a woman's mind, it changes like the weather.
(passing down the bag)
Catch it lad, this stallion is tearing at the tether.
(exit Cook, struggling with bag)
(to audience:)
I'll wager there was money there, and plenty more beside.
If I had turned my ears and just continued on my ride...

Fuel for my winter… the finest coat of wool,
You'd see the maids return my gaze then were my coffer full.
That was then, but now I see my wisdom came too late.
Let my blunder now remind you: never hesitate.

(Exit Horseman.)

SCENE 4

(A street scene, with a food stall.)

(Enter Vendor.)

NARRATOR
Behold our bold wayfaring waif will stop right here quite soon.
An hour since elevenses, he's flagging now by noon.
He's traipsed all morn and barely breached the outskirts of the city.
But know that pack bears sustenance, so spare him all your pity.

(Enter Cook.)

VENDOR
Eels' eggs! Fresh snails!
Cold stew! Boiled quails!

COOK
The sun is high, now let me eat a while here by this tree.
A mouth-watering banquet, sure, as it was cooked by… me!
One salmon, poached whole, fresh dill, and whole shallots,
The finest garden vegetables all sealed in little pots.
I'll have me only half the duck – roasted, flambéed then in rum

– But how to choose the right dessert? The best is yet to come!

VENDOR
Oi, here! You'll pay me now and thank me for the feast,
Or I'll call the law – you stole a shilling's worth at least!

COOK
Ah, gentle sir, how's business there? I wish a good day to you.
But here, I brought my own repast, pray what would I pay to you?

VENDOR
Rest you not to the north of me? Blows not the south breeze there?
The aroma from my kitchen, does it not sweetly bear?
And so you sit afeasting on the gorgeous homely smell.
You're happy pinching from me, but it does not suit me well.

COOK *(pauses to think, gets a shilling)*
Here is one bright shilling. See the shadow that I make?
   (puts it over Vendor's food and Vendor tries to take it)
That shadow should suffice for the aroma that I take!

(Exit Vendor.)

SCENE 5

(At a hermitage.)

NARRATOR
Afternoon was easy, belly full so baggage light.
He's reached the edge of Croydon now, and heavy draws the night.

He spies a little hut while seeking shelter from the cold.
He finds a door and taps, the gathering mist has made him bold.

(Enter Hermit from within.)

HERMIT
Pilgrim? Oh come in! I was expecting you today.
Yes, the constellations had it all mapped out that way.
Your bed is made, the stove is stoked, your welcome's unconditional.
Breakfast is included, yes – no charges are additional.
To improve my service, there's a box for your suggestions.
From my guest all I request is answers to three questions.
Three simple ones is all I ask, then you may pass the night.
Or get a healthy scolding if you fail to get them right.

COOK
Simple?

HERMIT
Yes.

COOK
'Tis chilly out, so…

HERMIT
Number one what's that? *(pointing to a cat)*

COOK
Despite its bandaged tail, I may still recognise a cat!

HERMIT
What? How dare you, man! That is no common household cat!

I'll knock some sense into you. Here, take that, and that, and that!
(beats the pilgrim)
Shame! It is Brigantis: Pagan goddess of the fire!
Come here and take that! So are you calling me a liar?
(suddenly composes himself)
Ready? Number two: now what is there inside the jug?

COOK
Easy sir, 'tis water! Do you take me for a mug?

HERMIT
Water? 'Tis my very life! My word how you offend.
(goes to beat him some more)

COOK
Oh silly! May I guess again? I s'ppose we could pretend.

HERMIT
Question three. You get this right and we'll forget the rest.
What's that up there? Now come on, this time please do try your best. *(points upwards)*
Well?

COOK
...Roof?

HERMIT
What?! There is the height of my good house!
Get out! Be gone and ne'er return until you grow more nous!

(Cook goes outside.)

COOK
No food, no bed, the way ahead now feels a world too far.
I'll have a smoke at least… what did I do with that cigar?

NARRATOR
So as the pilgrim calms his nerves and throws away the match,
The bandage wound around the feline's tail does fire catch,
And as she leaps upon the roof… I mean the house's height,
The bandage makes a kindle and the hut soon catches light.
A ragged smoky hermit then emerges from the blaze,
And seeking out the culprit, hand in punishment does raise.

COOK
Not so fast this time, it was your goddess of the fire!
Run and fetch your jug of life to rid her of her ire!

(Exeunt.)

SCENE 6

(On a Spanish road.)

(Enter Cook, appearing thinner.)

NARRATOR
Two months on, beyond now old Navarre and Castile.
Soon the well-trod path to Santiago will reveal
An ending to this road that spans the atmospheres and seasons.
One mind has weathered tests and choices, chances, tricks and reasons.
One heart burns pure and sure amidst the ugly and the sweet.
One body worn and blistered aches resisting its defeat.
One thought rings with the brightness of a sun. It is not fear,

Neither doubt nor observation, only thought: Why am I here?

(Virgin Mary appears in a vision.)

VIRGIN
Blessèd is the one resisting on his journey's course
All powers to dissuade him with their subtlety or force.
Blessèd one, arise. An empty goal has tied thee fast.
The purpose is the journey, from the first step to the last.
Is not thy love of God and love of life illumination?
'Tis time for you to turn about – home is your destination.
With newer eyes and stronger heart return now to your duty.
Through journeys the familiar can shed a deeper beauty.

(Exit Virgin Mary.)

COOK
Aye me, how I have waited long to feel a mother's love!
Now powersome, yet feather-soft, alighting from above.
How mighty and how glorious the faces of the Virgin.
Yet all the while a sweet familiarity emerging.
In a moment from those tender words were many aeons cast.
Let her guide, as she has guided: from the first step to the last!

(Exit Cook.)

SCENE 7

(The Duke's house.)

(Enter Duke and Duchess.)

DUKE
Darling, I love you, but these four walls will make me mad
As a rabid hound, so I beseech thee: grow not sad
In my absence, for in truth your failings are not relevant.
Keep your spirit... as your mother's build: stout as an elephant.

DUCHESS
Oh!

DUKE
But thou art seemly dear and must not lose an ounce
In pining for my presence, though your presence... I renounce.
I must leave! My joi de vivre has grown somewhat intransigent!

DUCHESS
Lord! How canst thy noble blood live on inside a mendicant?

(Enter Son.)

SON
Father, no! At least a little hut would you commission?
I shall design the stables and the lake with your permission.

DUCHESS
Perhaps on every Saturday this family could visit?
Thou shalt crave our presence! 'Tis no imposition... is it?

DUKE
Lord God, please have mercy on my poor reformèd soul!
Take me to the other world if not to my peaceful goal.

(Enter Virgin Mary.)

VIRGIN
Come, now board this chariot – thy life hast reached its end.
Away to other lives and days in solitude to spend.

(Exit Virgin Mary.)

DUKE
So late, but worse to never hear the call to spiritual life.

(Duke boards chariot.)

DUCHESS
My Lord, do await! Thou wouldst depart without thy wife?

(Duchess boards chariot.)

SON
Or leave me here an orphan – your one dear begotten son?
I'd be all alone here and it wouldn't be much fun!

(Son boards chariot. Enter Cook.)

COOK
Or send me to retirement? But you'll surely need a cook?

(Cook boards chariot. Chariot lurches about.)

DUKE
How unsure was our ascent, and how our carriage groaned and shook!
It shudders now and judders, and it whines under the weight!
It hosts too many passengers, but now it is too late… Aaargh!

(All fall to the ground and lie down, then Duke awakes and stands.)

How morbid and alarming to awake to one's own scream!
Yet soothing and delightful to discover it… a dream.

(Exit Duke, Duchess and Son.)

SCENE 8

(Outside the Duke's house.)

(Enter Stable Boy.)

STABLE BOY
So the wanderer returns… has he misplaced so many pounds?

COOK
Brother! Without you I'm as… the fox that slipped the hounds!

STABLE BOY
You are quite transfigured… though your garb remains unchanged. *(sniffs)*
We need a cook, without your skill the Duke is quite deranged!

COOK
More so!? How so? Then let me bathe here first.
Afore the day is closed you'll find him feasting fit to burst.

We'll revel 'til the morning, and you'll give me back my stash!

STABLE BOY
Why return? What have I safe?

COOK
A princely wad of cash.

STABLE BOY
The lunacy of pilgrimage still follows in your wake.
Can you produce a good receipt, or is there some mistake?

COOK
How could I take such proof from you my dearest, oldest friend?

STABLE BOY
Will we take the matter to the Duke, or fight until the end?

COOK *(laughing)*
Forgive! This weary form can scarce pursue you in your fun.

STABLE BOY
I jest not in this instance!

COOK *(sadly)*
...'Tis apparent... I'm undone.

(Enter Duke.)

DUKE
Firstly, who was witness to the dubious transaction?

COOK
None, Sire.

DUKE
None indeed, so we may take no further action.
Though it may serve to tell me whereabouts the scene took place.

COOK
By an oak tree.

DUKE
Oak? Then this is quite a simple case.
Ask the oak for evidence, and bring to me its word.

STABLE BOY
Sire, it is a tree! The mere suggestion is absurd.

DUKE *(to Cook)*
Do it!

COOK *(exiting)*
Sire.

STABLE BOY
My Lord, I fear he may be quite some while.
'Tis through the yard and pastures by the gatekeeper's wood pile.

DUKE
You know the tree, you scoundrel! Find the money and return it!

STABLE BOY
I earned it well by guarding it! Return? I'd sooner burn it!

DUKE
Do it! Then you may well keep your post in my employ.
And whilst you're busy fetching things, return the pilgrim boy.

(Exit Stable Boy, enter Cook with money.)

COOK
Sire, to thee once more I am most humbly in debt.

DUKE
Hm! Choose your friends more wisely: those with fewer traps to set.
Boy, now heed my word: I've long admired your dedication.
But something brighter in your face now fires my inspiration.
This news may well astound you, but despite my first reaction
Your pilgrimage – the simple life – now grows in its attraction.
My doubts are cast asunder by the brilliance in your eyes.
Though sans a school certificate… I warrant thou art wise.
These legs are far to agèd to embark on pilgrimage,
I am for the forest bound to build a hermitage.
Perhaps there simply comes a day
For each man, when the soul holds sway.
A new man then would burst to burgeon!
With a vastness merge and
Fly abroad from comforts itchy!
The cosy, of a sudden… twitchy!

NARRATOR
Friends, we hope this little play has garnered your attention.
We dedicate it to you, names too numerous to mention.
Forgive us any errors, let us harbour no misgiving.

We only seek to bring a dash of joy to light your living.
We salute the pilgrim in the heart of each one's being,
Who knows the art of living is in feeling, not just seeing.
With merriment and company we'll lighten all the load.
Behold, the journey beckons us! Come, let us greet the road!

3
MIRABAI

BASED ON THE STORIES BY SRI CHINMOY:

CHILD'S LOVE FOR GOD [8]
OF THE SAME CASTE [9]
YOU ARE WORSE THAN A GHOST [10]
THE SON OF AN ASS [11]
THE DISTANCE BETWEEN TRUTH AND FALSEHOOD [12]
THE FOOLISH AND THE WISE [13]
HEAVEN AND HELL [14]
AKBAR, TANSEN AND HARIDAS [15]
AKBAR'S SECRET VISIT TO MIRABAI [16]

Inspired by the talk:
MUSIC AND RELIGION [17]

CAST

KRISHNA
MIRABAI
MIRABAI'S FATHER, RATNA SINGH
MIRABAI'S MOTHER
AKBAR THE GREAT
BIRBAL (AKBAR'S MINISTER AND JESTER)
MIRABAI'S HUSBAND, PRINCE BHOJA RAJ
MIRABAI'S MOTHER-IN-LAW
MIRABAI'S SISTER-IN-LAW
TANSEN
HARIDAS (TANSEN'S TEACHER)
NARRATOR

First performed in Antalya, Turkey
January 3rd 2007

SCENE 1

(At the palace, parental home of Mirabai.)

(Enter Mirabai, with Krishna as a statue.)

NARRATOR
The honeyed sun came closer to,
But shyly veiled himself from view,
Drawing spices from the air.
The maiden moon watched soft and fair.
Early stars came out to glisten.
Bells and creatures stilled to listen.
   (Mirabai's music starts)
Tiger harkened out of sight,
Peacock nestled for the night,
Spider paused upon his yarn.
The young princess of Rajasthan,
Sweeter, finer than them all,
Sang behind a jewelled wall.

(Enter Mother and Father. Mirabai still sings.)

FATHER *(furious)*
If I see that Moghul scum
In ten miles of my country come,
That rank Mohammedan I'll curse
With fleas or warts or death, or worse!
I'll pluck his whiskers one by one!
I'll light his hair to see him run!
I'll skin his ears, I'll roast his eyes!
Can any Hindu man despise
That rogue Akbar more than I do?
And what gives *her* the freedom to *(points at Mirabai)*

Just sing and prattle all her life?
She is soon to be the wife
Of Bhoja Raj, the future king!
Will he want to hear her *sing*!?
Have you wondered how we'll look
If this our daughter cannot cook,
Wear proper dress, or serve him tea?

MOTHER
Shanti! Dearest, let her be.
Krishna is her only love.
Her marriage vows came from above.
You may think her pale and odd,
But all she does, she does for God.
How can we send our child away
When all she knows is how to pray?
Her fate is sealed, her path is set.

FATHER *(more furious)*
I command her to forget
That ever she was Mirabai
And idled here with you and I!
I'll make her overcome this fad,
Before that statue drives her mad!
Her only way to win my pride
Is as a Hindu warrior's bride!

(Exit parents, Mother crying. Mirabai continues to sing, then exits with Krishna.)

SCENE 2

(At Akbar's palace.)

(Sounds of Akbar and Birbal laughing, and a dog barking off stage. Enter Akbar and Birbal, laughing.)

AKBAR
Birbal, can you tell me how
Your dog comes to ignore you now?
He wagged his tail and begged for food.
The plate I gave was half as good
As that you offered next to mine,
Yet yours he shunned, and chose to dine
Exclusively upon my fare!

BIRBAL
My king, that dog would not beware
A single morsel from my hand
No matter what its taste or brand.
His choice came not from his suspicion.
Even dogs know their position:
With his *kind* he takes repast –
He's always faithful to his caste!

(They laugh and Akbar chases Birbal.)

AKBAR
Birbal, you scamp, you imp, you knave!
Now I will *force* you to behave,
And I will go to any length! *(grabs Birbal by the wrist)*
So you demon, show your strength!
If you escape from Akbar's grip,
You will avoid his horse's whip!

BIRBAL *(not trying to escape)*
Rama! Rama! Rama! Rama!
Rama! Rama! Rama! Rama!

AKBAR
What? You chant instead of fight?
How will that loose a grip so tight?

BIRBAL
When one is haunted by a ghost,
It's Rama's name that helps the most.
Ghosts are scared and soon turn tail,
But with you it seems to fail…
You are no ghost, you must be worse!
Who'll free me from this fateful curse?

(Akbar promptly releases him.)

AKBAR
I'm not worse! It's me, your king,
With whom you play and sport and sing!
O dearest friend, O noble minister,
Do you think your Akbar sinister?
   (Birbal laughs and runs away)
And so I see you win again!
You are the cleverest of men.
But, rascal, pixie, gremlin, monkey!
Come here, you son of a… donkey!

BIRBAL *(laughing)*
Ah! Yes, now your words are true.
Your Majesty, none else but you
Could I consider my true father,
And no other would I rather.

AKBAR
Truth is false and false is fair!
Ah, Birbal, I do despair!
They are too close to see the difference!

BIRBAL
Here, three inches is the distance
From what's false to what is true.
Let me demonstrate on you.
Fibs and gossip we may hear,
These all enter through the ear.
Here's the place that knows no lies,
As only truth enters the eyes!

AKBAR
Oh Birbal, you're the wisest fool,
You teach me more than any school.

BIRBAL
No Majesty, no fool is wise.
A fool is one who never tries
To make his work on earth complete.
His life again he must repeat,
Until he sees his duty done.
The wise man's worldly goal is won
By finishing what he has started.
He'll not return once he's departed
From this outer earthly plane.
But that does not quite explain
Who goes to Heaven or to hell.
That finer point I've yet to tell.
The truly wise are those whose birth
Brings only love to all on earth.

They see God in all creation:
Every heart and every nation.
Therefore, *you* are truly wise.
This is no sycophantic praise.
You love the Christians and the Jews,
You always ask me for their news.
Of the Hindu and the Sikh,
Only highly do you speak.
You love those who don't give love:
Like the cow, the pig, the dove,
The dog, you'd even love the fleas.
The dawn, the dusk, the rain, the breeze –
All is Godly in your sight.
The one who loves is always right.

AKBAR
Birbal, I'm again disarmed.
With your heart my heart you've charmed.
Now I'm stumped, I'm stunned, I'm beat….
So let us use our mouths to eat!

(Exit both, laughing.)

SCENE 3

(At the palace, marital home of Mirabai.)

(Mirabai follows Bhoja Raj around the fire to a sacred chant and they garland each other, signifying their marriage. Mother-In-Law greets them and all three exit. Mirabai re-enters, crosses the stage with Krishna and prays. Enter Sister-In-Law and Mother-In-Law.)

SISTER-IN-LAW
No, I will not call her sister!
The word would give my tongue a blister!
I'd rather give a good hard kick!
So meek and pure, she makes me sick!
She has you round her little finger.
Face it, she's a dreadful singer.
Piggy eyes, her nose is small,
She's ugly and she's much too tall.
She snubs the goddess that we worship,
Worst of all she does not *gossip*!

MOTHER-IN-LAW
You've taunted Mirabai enough!
Everybody has their stuff.
It's time you cut the girl some slack.
She's here and we can't send her back.
Beside that, we could use the dowry.
I tried to make her pray to Gauri,
She just begged me for that statue.
"Fine," I said, "But if I catch you
Sleeping past the break of day
Because you sang the night away,
I'll eat you whole, so woe betide you!
Then your Krishna will not hide you!"

(Mother-In-Law exits laughing. Enter Bhoja Raj.)

SISTER-IN-LAW
Brother, do you think your wife
Will love and serve you all her life,
Baking cakes and knitting slippers,
Fetching you your morning kippers?
You think that she prays all night,

That all she does is sweet and right.
Well brother, I'm a super-sleuth –
I followed her to find the truth.
She's in the temple sure enough,
But not to pray – that's all a bluff!
She meets in there with other men!
She turns the place into a den,
Drinking, dancing all night long.
It's base, perverse... and very wrong!

(Bhoja Raj runs to the other side of the stage with his sword bared, listening at the temple. Exit Sister-In-Law, laughing.)

MIRABAI
Krishna, stray not from my sight,
No one understands my plight.
I am mad with love for you,
All else is obscured from view.
Fire rages in my heart
For you alone. I cannot part
From that which is my very soul.
Your heart's joy is my only goal.

BHOJA RAJ *(laughing, shaking head, exiting)*
Oh my sister is a tyke!
Deadpan, straight-faced as you like,
Claiming Mirabai's impure.
Pigs would fly first, now I'm sure.

(Exit Mirabai and Krishna.)

SCENE 4

(At Akbar's palace.)

(Enter Akbar and Tansen. Tansen starts to play sitar.)

AKBAR *(crying)*
Ah, Tansen, your notes are gems!
They'd charm the lilies from their stems,
Each as sweet as any cherry,
They would make a deaf man merry!
Tansen, there's no competition,
I say you're the best musician.

TANSEN
Majesty, if that were true,
I would not come to play for you.
The best are best because they know
Their talent is not meant for show.
The best will play for God alone –
They live in forests on their own,
In wooden hovels rude and bare.
For palaces they have no care,
But not for me that lonesome hush!
I adore this royal plush –
Marble walls and crystal fountains,
Minarets beneath the mountains,
Plates of sweets in every room,
Fresh towels with their light perfume,
Little cakes all drenched in honey...
No, I play for fame and money,
But two others you must hear –
Their notes are chocolate for the ear.
They still the tiger, lure the dove,

Conquer storms and conjure love!
Because their notes are the Supreme's,
Their music is beyond my dreams.
They are my teacher Haridas
And Mirabai, the young princess.
I will take you to each place,
But first we'll somehow change your face.
I will take you as my slave,
But worry not, you needn't shave.
We'll wrap you up in some old swathe
And tell them you've just been to bathe,
Or that you fear the light of day...
Or that you always dress that way.

AKBAR
No, you jest! Can this be true?
Both superior to you?
I'll surely drown in my own tears!
Let me hear with my own ears.

(Exit both. Enter Haridas, sitting down to meditate. Enter Akbar, disguised, with Tansen. Tansen folds hands and touches the feet of Haridas.)

TANSEN
Master Haridas, pranam,
The sight of you is such a balm.
I have brought a man today
Whose dream is just to hear you play. *(hands him a sitar)*
In fact this is his last desire
Before he greets his funeral pyre.
He is so frail and very old, *(Akbar stoops)*
And now dementia's taking hold. *(Akbar wanders vaguely)*
I promised him this final meeting.

Will you bless him with a greeting?
He's a worker in my house,
Completely free of flea and louse,
Just some diseases of the skin. *(Akbar starts scratching)*
Won't you permit him to come in?

HARIDAS
Let the old man have a seat!
Don't let him stoop to touch my feet.
Would he like a cup of tea?
But why would you bring him to me?
I thought you would have had more sense –
I never take an audience!
Let him hear what you have gained
In all those years of being trained
According to the ancient ways.
Show him how a master plays,
As everything I ever knew
I have in turn bestowed on you.
Come, my son, I'll listen proudly.
Play it well, and play it loudly. *(carefully hands back the sitar)*

(Bluegrass music. Tansen plays it like a banjo, jumping around the stage. Haridas covers his ears, then tries to grab Tansen.)

HARIDAS
Aaagh, Tansen! Are you insane?!
Ohhh how my ears cry in pain!
What beast or devil is within you?
My Tansen? Can it be true?
God above, do please protect him!
A plague of bluegrass does infect him! *(takes the sitar)*
I must insist you let me play,
To wash that dreadful sound away!

(Haridas plays as he exits in ecstasy. Akbar and Tansen follow, jubilant. Enter Mirabai and Krishna. She starts to sing. Enter Akbar and Tansen.)

AKBAR
Ah, it's sweeter than a bird –
Than any music ever heard
By this or any other ear!
Strong, yet delicate and clear.
I feel my soul has taken flight
Upon the very sound's delight,
Captured by its upward drift…
Before we go, I leave this gift.
These diamonds are a tiny token
Of the praise my heart has spoken.

(Akbar carefully puts a diamond necklace at the foot of Krishna. Exit Akbar and Tansen. Music fades. Enter Bhoja Raj, who grabs the necklace.)

BHOJA RAJ
You bring a scandal on our race!
You let a Muslim see your face!?
Accepting from him lavish jewels,
And singing to him while he drools?
Where's your female modesty,
Your sense, your shame, your honesty?
He's your father's greatest rival!
Don't you care for our survival?
Take *pride* in Hindu sovereignty!
Are you devoid of enmity,
Of wisdom, judgement and perception?
You'd give each creed the same reception?!
You are not fit to share my crown –

Not fit to live… so you must *drown*!
Your proper place, O base deceiver,
Is at the bottom of a river!

(Exit Bhoja Raj.)

SCENE 5

(At a river. River sounds.)

MIRABAI
Krishna, leave me not alone.
I've no virtue of my own.
Be my virtue, and my crown
Or in this torrent shall I drown!
Save my honour, take this life.
Never have I been a wife
Except in constancy to you.
Take me, if this heart is true.
   (Krishna comes to life, river sounds subside, flute music plays)
On a sudden comes the sight…
Stills all, your look of light!
Unbreakable, my Lord, the love
That bound me here to you above.
In you shall I go on living
Far beyond this unforgiving
World of sorrow, heartless, cruel.
Like the lotus in the pool
In you alone can I exist.
The world beyond will be our tryst.

(Exit Krishna and Mirabai together.)

4
KRISHNA'S VICTORY

BASED ON THE STORIES BY SRI CHINMOY:
KRISHNA'S SUPREME LOVE [18]
TWO DIVINE LIARS: ARE THEY REALLY SO? [19]
THE THEFT OF THE SYAMANTAK DIAMOND [20]

CAST

KRISHNA
DEVAKI (KRISHNA'S MOTHER)
SATYAVAMA (KRISHNA'S WIFE)
BALARAMA (KRISHNA'S BROTHER)
KING KANGSA (KRISHNA'S UNCLE)
KANGSA'S MINISTER
AKRURA (KRISHNA'S UNCLE, SERVES KANGSA)
DURVASHA (A GREAT SAGE)
DEMON
NARRATOR

First performed in Varna, Bulgaria
January 10th 2007

PROLOGUE

(Enter Devaki.)

NARRATOR
Who weeps behind the dismal prison gate?
Whose inner might could yet survive this fate?
Six sons she bore, but each before first breath
Was snatched away and hurled unto his death.
What deeper pain than this could smite a mother?
Much worse, this hell was dealt by her own brother.
Six jewels of the mighty Yadav clan
Were culled at birth by their own uncle's hand.

(Enter Balarama.)

The seventh, so the hoary legend went,
Was by some magic to another sent –
Great Balaram escaped an early tomb
By entering a second mother's womb.
The eighth was Uncle Kangsa's only dread:

(Enter Krishna.)

This nephew, so the ancient sages said,
Would be the cause of Kangsa's bitter end.
Upon that infant's death did he depend,
But little did he know the mighty soul
In tiny form would thwart his evil goal.
The newborn to a foster mother fled,
To wear a peacock crown upon his head.

(Exeunt.)

SCENE 1

(At Kangsa's palace.)

(Enter Kangsa and Minister.)

MINISTER *(bowing excessively)*
Dear King, you are the pinnacle of virtue!
Pray let no subtle quality desert you.
Each movement and inflection so refined –
The product of a pure, uncluttered mind.
All Heaven's angels fall before your feet!
Your radiant smile transfigures all you meet,
Your eyes of truth themselves engender trust!
And… let me see… your crown so… free from… rust.

KANGSA
Enough, you fawning, crawling toady worm,
As bright and charismatic as a… germ!
Did I ask you to bow and lie to me,
Or is your job to seek my enemy?

MINISTER
Ah… yes… of course, I quite forgot to say –
I happened to discover him today.
In Brindaban he sings and plays and… whirls
Amongst a seething mass of pretty girls
And he…

KANGSA
Get back there, I need him dead!
Don't come back here without Sri Krishna's head!

(Exeunt.)

SCENE 2

(At Brindaban.)

(Enter Krishna, playing the flute. Enter Minister.)

MINISTER
Aha! You're caught, don't try to run away!
　(Krishna stops playing, but stays motionless, listening)
Uncharismatic cur, you've had your day!
I've seen you sporting here with all your… 'wives'.
I might well put an end to all *their* lives!
　(gestures to female audience)
I'm known throughout the land as Ruthless Jake
Due to the quantity of lives I take,
With cunning and a cruel imagination.
Destruction is far finer than creation,
It is my art – by death my blood is stirred,
As execution has the final word.
My weapon is a marvel to behold.
How swift am I, and sleek and sly and bold.
Enough of me though, it's your special day!
Now Ruthless Jake has spied your sordid play!
These youthful maidens flocking in their droves,
Entranced and fawning, trembling like doves
Each time you play a note or glance their way.
They dance and curl beside you night and day.
You're known throughout this land for inner height.
The truth is you're a slur, a burr, a blight,
A blot, a clot, a germ, a worm, carbuncle.
So Ruthless Jake was sent here by your uncle
To cleanse this kingdom of your sinful game,
And finally erase your filthy name!
My blade is quick, there's no time for a fight.

(Krishna kills him immediately.)

KRISHNA
But not as quick as divine justice-light.
I listened and forgave them all these years.
It seems my silence fell upon deaf ears.
  (to female audience:)
My love for you some will not comprehend,
But always your dear hearts my heart will tend.
You will remain beyond the world's commotion,
By sheltering inside your true devotion.

(Exeunt.)

SCENE 3

(At Kangsa's palace.)

(Enter Kangsa and Akrura.)

KANGSA
Akrura, now my anger is torrential!
Your time has come – unlock your deep potential.
Brute force has failed, you must in gentle ways
Release me from these wretched haunted days.
I am his uncle, you his uncle too,
But seems he has a softer spot for you.
I'll honour him now with a splendid tournament.
Bedeck the scene with drape and jewel and ornament,
Let many kings recline on silk divans,
Ten slaves apiece to pamper them with fans,
In feathered hats and shining leather boots.
Bring honeyed wine and out-of-season fruits.

Bring Krishna and his brother Balaram.
Be kind, polite and milder than a lamb.
For Balaram some demon I'll employ,
Sri Krishna with my own hand I'll destroy!

(Exeunt.)

SCENE 4

(At Brindaban.)

(Enter Krishna and Balarama. Enter Akrura.)

KRISHNA
Good uncle! Now this day is truly blessed –
In Brindaban Akrura takes his rest.
Do have some butter... or a cup of chai?
But why so pale? And how you frown and sigh.

AKRURA
You are my nephew but you are my Lord.
By this heart and the world you are adored.
Excepting one: my cruel, deranged employer.
His only goal: to be my Lord's destroyer.
He's staging some great tournament for you,
But he will kill you and your brother too.
He'll muster thugs who've mastered nasty tricks.
This so-called tournament is all a fix.
King Kangsa plans to fight you to the end.

KRISHNA
Akrura, dearest uncle, greatest friend,
To your great loyalty I am in debt.

This fealty my heart will not forget.
Come Balaram, to Uncle Kangsa's house!
Hah! Would the lion quake before the mouse?

(Exit Akrura.)

SCENE 5

(At Kangsa's palace.)

(Enter Kangsa and a demon. Krishna kills Kangsa, Balaram kills the demon.)

(Exeunt.)

SCENE 6

(At Krishna's palace.)

(Enter Krishna and Satyavama. Enter Durvasha, beyond a river, meditating.)

SATYAVAMA
My Lord, it is the lowest crime and shame!
Your greatest devotee repeats your name
Day in, day out, in constant adoration.
Can you not show him your appreciation?
It is beyond a mere lack of respect –
No, all you give him is your cruel neglect.
He only lives on grass – one blade or two.
He starves and suffers all because of you.
Can you not ask someone to bring him food?

KRISHNA
Meals will never do him any good...
But as you wish, go make him some chapattis.

SATYAVAMA
And dahl, and little spicy chickpea patties,
Salt lassi, rice with cardamoms and almonds,
...And for dessert... a dozen gulab jamuns.

(Satyavama goes to the river with the food. Krishna shrugs then resumes playing the flute.)

Alas, the gentle Jamuna is wild!
On other days she babbles like a child,
Silk-softly flow the ripples of her gown,
But now a thousand elephants she'd drown!
The ferry-boat will not survive her anger,
But meanwhile poor Durvasha aches with hunger.
    (returns to Krishna)
My Lord, I cannot go, the river's furious!

KRISHNA
Indeed? The gentle Jamuna? How curious...
Well, God will not forgive me if you drown.
Go, tell the river that she must calm down
Providing my next statement is all true:
No woman in the world apart from you
Has this, your Krishna, ever looked upon.

SATYAVAMA
What will the river do? This is a con!
You know you've seen a thousand female faces
Right here, in Brindaban and other places.
Were your dear gopis men or womenfolk?

…I see this is no time for me to joke.
My Lord, I must obey you, here I go. *(returns to the river)*
Great Jamuna, now you must calm your flow
Assuming Krishna's eyes have never seen
The face of any woman but this queen.
   (river calms and she crosses)
Durvasha, I have brought you food at last!
Now Satyavama bids you break your fast.

DURVASHA
I'm blessed! I sensed today would be auspicious.
   (starts to eat)
Ah, Mother Satyavama, it's delicious!
Your kind concern has fed my soul each day,
And now you feed my life in every way.
It's more good-fortune than I dare believe!

SATYVAMA
Enjoy the gulabs, I must take my leave.
My Krishna soon will worry I am lost.
   (goes to the river)
Another storm descended since I crossed!
   (returns to Durvasha)
Durvasha, I can't go, the river's furious!

DURVASHA
Indeed? The gentle Jamuna? How curious.
Well, God will not forgive me if you drown.
Go, tell the river that she must calm down
And make the crossing safe again for you,
Providing my next statement is all true:
That this Durvasha's eaten only grass
Since all the last ten years have come to pass.

SATYAVAMA
Durvasha! But you know that is not true.
All six chapattis were consumed by you
Not half an hour ago upon this spot,
Right here before my eyes, have you forgot?
...I'm stranded so I see I have no choice.
But how the lie will tremble in my voice!
Lord Krishna, please protect me, here I go. *(returns to the river)*
Good Jamuna, now you must calm your flow
If Sage Durvasha has maintained his fast
C... *completely* while the last decade has passed.
  (river calms, she crosses and goes to Krishna)
I thought you stood for truth! Please tell me why
You've taught your greatest devotee to lie?
Am I the only woman you have seen?
Has Sage Durvasha eaten not one bean?
He ate a banquet whole before my eyes!

KRISHNA
My dearest, so the highest truth is lies?
Durvasha ate but did not *taste* your food.
A shame – it must be said your cooking's good.
No, he resolved to diet upon leaves,
So that's the only taste his mouth receives.
Durvasha lives beyond the earthly plane,
Devoid of pleasure, preference or pain.
All earthly food is grass, or so he thinks.
It's only divine nectar that he drinks.
He lives on Heaven's ecstasy-delight.
See now that the Jamuna was right?
You are the mother of this blossoming world.
Long since the primal flora first unfurled
You dreamed within the seemly modest moon,
Your gaze the grace of one perpetual boon,

The author and protector of each child,
The might within the sweet, the soft and mild.
Mysterious, wondrous power of creation,
All blooms and thrives within your meditation.
You are as one with me – my female part.
Whom can I see when you are in my heart?
To me you occupy each woman's place,
And so in truth I only see your face.
Come now! You must be hungry from your walk.
Let's eat some gulab jamun while we talk.

(They eat, then Satyavama opens and reads a letter.)

SATYAVAMA
My Lord, I've bitter news: my father's dead!
Foul Shatdhanwa killed him in his bed!
More tragic: he was murdered for a *jewel*.
What jealous greed could make a man so cruel?
The diamond named Syamantak issued gold
To all my father's ancestors of old.
And each of those whose hands fall on that gem
Have countless coins of gold bestowed on them.
But now my father's gone, that jewel is mine,
And only in this palace should it shine.
Lord Krishna, please avenge my father's end.
This grave injustice only you can mend.

KRISHNA
Foul Shatdhanwa, you will feel my fury!
Now I shall be the court, the judge and jury,
And death will be the sentence for your deed!
No other penalty can match your greed!

(Exeunt.)

SCENE 7

(In a forest.)

(Enter Akrura, meditating. Enter Krishna, running and searching.)

What can I do? He's swifter than a deer.
I'm sure I saw him running right through here.
No sooner do I see him than he's fled.
I will not stop until I see him dead.
I'll scour the fields and forests of Mathura.
But wait, is that my good Uncle Akrura
Lost deep within a meditative trance?
   (picks up diamond from his lap)
And look at this, what strange and happy chance,
The jewel I seek is nestled in his lap!
How can this be? Perhaps it is a trap?

AKRURA
My Krishna? Is it you, so far from home?

KRISHNA
For vengeance and for justice do I roam!
Dear Satyavama's father has been killed.
I cannot rest until I have fulfilled
My duties as her husband and her king.
But he was murdered for this very thing. *(holds up diamond)*
Good uncle, can you help me understand
How this great diamond came into your hand?

AKRURA
I was just meditating by this tree,
And someone dropped the jewel onto my knee.
Before I saw his face he ran away.

But more than that I truly cannot say.

KRISHNA
Akrura, will you keep it now it's yours?

AKRURA
No! Greed has brought this planet only wars!
It comes from Satyavama's family line.
How can I now consider it as mine?
Since you and she are one, it's yours to keep.

(Krishna takes the diamond.)

KRISHNA
What blessing can reward a heart so deep?
Yours is a selfless, unconditional heart.
I know you've been on God's Side from the start.
A boon, Akrura, to you I shall give.

AKRURA *(touching Krishna's feet)*
My Lord, it is enough for me to live
This sacred incarnation here beside you.
As all my goodness started from inside you,
If I take all the credit, I'm a fool.
I know you neither need me nor this jewel!
I'm blessed that I have lived to serve you twice.

KRISHNA
For this devotion there can be no price.
Yes, friends I have, dear ones, admirers too,
But nowhere else a devotee like you.

5
THE PRINCESS AND THE PIRATE

BASED ON THE STORIES BY SRI CHINMOY:

THE SAILOR AND THE PARROT [21]
LIGHT IS THE ONLY WEALTH WORTH HAVING [22]

CAST

PIRATE VENTURO
KING
QUEEN
PRINCESS FORTUNA
DUCHESS FIFI
DUCHESS MIMI
PRIME MINISTER
PRINCE ADMIRAL ALPHONSE
SAILOR 1
SAILOR 2
MONK 1
MONK 2
ANGEL

SET IN 18th CENTURY SOUTHERN EUROPE

First performed in Bali, Indonesia
February 8th 2009

ACT 1, SCENE 1

(At the palace.)

(Enter Pirate Venturo, secretly, hiding behind thrones. Enter King and Queen, followed by Prime Minister.)

KING
Minister, what news today of life beyond our borders?
Make it brief, the chef is soon to come and take our orders,
Then we have a manicure at twenty-five past ten.

QUEEN
Probably when that is done we'll need to eat again.
Surely it is splendid sport to reign as queen and king,
But leaves short time for long reports, much less for idling.
Speak up now, the King's new hair does so affect his hearing.

PRIME MINISTER *(very clearly)*
Majesties, a war is closer than I have been fearing.
To this matter I entreat your full and close attention.
Yes, the King's new periwig does first deserve a mention –
The royal visage is within it admirably framed –
But I dread the noble head beneath it may be claimed.
Inside a year I dare predict a southerly invasion,
Our small nation does not look so well in that equation.
For your safety I must urge a northerly alliance –
Unlike manicures, the matter can afford no dalliance.
I propose a marriage match between Princess Fortuna
And Prince Admiral Alphonse, within six months or sooner.
As your only daughter the Princess's role is crucial.
Her virtues and her lineage will make the profit mutual.
Prince Alphonse is first in line to the North Empire's throne.
Love of gamb'ling and a love of wine we must condone.

Politics and leadership go quite above his head.
Let's focus on his... bravery and... gallantry instead,
His stature and his... wit are sure to claim her fair young heart.
With your blessing certainly her hand would be a start.
Say you hold a ball for him tomorrow tonight, or sooner.
There involve the Duchesses and fair Princess Fortuna,
There the navy fleet will have their joy of jolly dancing,
There the merry music and the finest wine enhancing
All the many merits of our small but noble land.
Before the night has played its last, the Prince will ask her hand,
Then our countries – major and the minor – will be one.
Pardon please my musical and quite amusing pun.

KING *(to Queen)*
What was that he said my dear? I hardly caught a word.
Something about dancing and the finest wine I heard.
He's indeed a lovely man, his waistcoats are fantastic,
But in speech he mumbles and his style is so... bombastic.

(Venturo listens to conversation, steals ornament from the Queen's hair and exits.)

QUEEN *(loudly and deliberately)*
Dear, this little land of ours is in a spot of danger.
If we treat the Northern Empire as a foe or stranger
We'll be swallowed from the south... in some unpleasant way,
So he says we must not waste a single night or day.
In order to avert this irreversible calamity,
We'll approach the northern lands with courtesy and amity,
Offer to the Northern Emperor's son our only daughter,
Thus the matter's settled well, as blood's thicker than water.

Nat'rally the north will give their full and sure protection
Against a brute intrusion from a southerly direction.
So at once we must induce a favourable response
From the northern – dashing brave – Prince Admiral
   Alphonse.

KING
So we hold a splendid ball at once with jolly dancing,
There the merry music and the finest wine enhancing

KING AND PRIME MINISTER
All the many merits of our small but noble land.

KING
That I heard! And then the Prince will surely ask her hand –
Wizard! Corking! Cracking! What a super duper plan.
There will not have been a finer ball since… time began.
I do love these good excuses for a proper bash.
So much to prepare my dear, come, come, now we must dash!

(Exeunt.)

ACT 1, SCENE 2

(At the palace.)

(Enter Queen, followed by Fortuna, followed by the Duchesses, all wearing additional masks. Fifi pauses to take a cake.)

QUEEN
Come Fortuna! Now employ your finest regal charms.
Your land's fate depends upon the way you hold your arms,
And maybe hold your tongue throughout the evening for a

change –
I fear these northern gentlemen may find your accent strange.
Stand up straight, but gracefully, chin up, that's it, eyes
    down,
Smile in moderation, but don't let me see you frown.
Tread as if your feet are downy feathers on the floor.
It's up to you now to avert this nuisance of a war.
Duchess Mimi! Try to match your cousin's good behaviour.
Duchess Fifi! Manners now could be this country's saviour.
Do not take the sweets or cakes and thus outgrow your dress!
Now excuse me for a while, the King's hair is a mess.

(Exit Queen.)

FORTUNA
Cousins, I can scarcely breathe in my anticipation!
That we'll meet the northern fleet defies imagination.

FIFI
I heard Prince Alphonse is stronger than a dozen men.
Once he swam to Tuscany and then… straight back again!
All the while he held aloft a standard in one hand
Displaying his own Navy crest!

MIMI
I cannot understand
What drives a man to strive for so much valiance and strength.
Seems in feats of daring some will go to any length.
Once I heard he felled a tree with one stroke of his sword.
With that self-same implement he shaved it to a board
With which to plug a gaping hole beneath his own ship's helm.
This, I warn you ladies, may your senses overwhelm:
He dove beneath the ocean and repaired it in one breath!
A full ten minutes – any man would sooner meet his death!

FIFI
Yes, and his heroic heart of goodness never fails.
What about the time he saved a family of whales
That one by one had accidentally wandered to the shore.
Here I must confess I've never seen a whale before,
But I've heard they're even bigger than our royal yacht.
Dauntless though, the Prince Alphonse was out there like a shot.
On his shoulders lifted he each one without commotion,
And gently placed it – belly downwards – back into the ocean.

MIMI
Hush! The Prince's entourage is on its way I think!

(Mimi listens stage left. Enter Prince Alphonse and Sailors stage left to a sailing song.)

FIFI
Oh, my hands are trembling! Wait there, I need a drink.

(Runs away stage left, accidentally toward the entourage.)

PRINCE ALPHONSE *(in a Yorkshire accent)*
Land ahoy, me'hearties! Let's bring down the anchor here.
   (to Fifi)
What a pretty thing have we? What is your name, my dear?

FIFI
Fff F… Fifi

PRINCE ALPHONSE
A little minuet I'm sure would see your stutters calmed.
Find me later, I can guarantee you won't be harmed.
   (Mimi tries to pull Fifi away)

And, who's this? I see we have an even brighter gem
That glitters as divinely as on Heaven's diadem.

MIMI
Mimi

PRINCE ALPHONSE
You, yes. You stammer like your sister, come on don't be wary;
My combat skills are legend, but with ladies I'm not scary.
We'll talk about it later then, you needn't be alarmed.

(Enter Queen hurriedly dragging King along, adjusting his hair.)

QUEEN
Prince Alphonse! Your Highness, by your presence we are charmed.
Please enjoy the feasting and the drinking and the dance.
Though it is a masked ball, I won't leave one thing to chance:
That fair young lady standing in the pale and seemly dress
Is our heir and daughter, our Fortuna, the Princess!

PRINCE ALPHONSE
Yes, a regal bearing, I can sense it from afar.
In this glowing galaxy she shines the brightest star.
  (Fortuna approaches timidly to join the Duchesses)
Majesties, how charmed am I to have your invitation.
As a rule I only socialise in moderation,
  (Sailor 1 coughs)
But your timing's perfect, for I'm seldom found at home.
  (Sailor 1 nods)
An Admiral – as I am – was forever born to roam.
I am dedicated to my country's preservation!
Saving lives has always been my foremost aspiration.
  (Fifi swoons, Mimi catches)

And... taking them, of course, whenever circumstance
   dictates.
I am setting sail tomorrow – with my merry mates –
On a swashbu-ck-ling and extremely dangerous quest.
I must rid this planet of the one I most detest!
The infamous Venturo, pirate of the southern seas
Was spotted by my lookout in the Channel of Belize,
So at dawn we leave to cross the perilous Atlantic.
As you can imagine, my dear mother will be frantic,
But the foul Venturo has adventured long enough.
Now it's time to show him Alphonse also can play tough!
   (Mimi swoons, Fifi catches)

QUEEN
Oh! Belize! My goodness, would you go to such a length?
There are many... closer... places to display your... strength,
All for just one pirate? Is a he really such a threat?

PRINCE ALPHONSE
Yes, it is essential, for my honour is in debt!
First he ransacked all the wealthy harbours of the north,
Pillaging and plundering and looting back and forth,
Then broke into my father's vault and stole his favourite crown,
Like a shadow in the night. I never tracked him down –
He always lurks one step before me in his wicked fun.
This time I will show him all his trickery is done.

QUEEN
But... the weather will be turning dreadful overnight,
Are you certain it is wise to take such sudden flight?
You may meet your peril if you take that weighty chance!
Wait until you taste our wine! Now come and start the dance.

(Exeunt.)

ACT 1, SCENE 3

(At the palace.)

(Enter Fortuna – centre – and Duchesses – left and right, facing away – each reading letters privately to themselves.)

MIMI
Mimi,

FORTUNA
Fortuna,

FIFI
Fifi,

VOICE OF PRINCE ALPHONSE
Dearest, since I met you I have been in quite a trance,
Remembering in detail every step of our last dance.
I'm a blinded man now, one who looks but never sees,
My eyes are for you only, even here in bright Belize.
My heart is only yours, and I would send it in a jar.
Can you hear it beating for you even from afar?
Without you I'm like a... cracker that has lost its cheese,
A ship without a... shipment, or a forest without trees.
Every day I catch a... fish and name it after you,
Every night I make a wish and... wish it will come true:
That in a month I may return and look upon your face.
Truly you must know that nobody could take your place.
Signed by Prince Algernon Derek Reginald Alphonse,
Ardently awaiting your alacritous response.
(Mimi and Fifi roll up their letters and exit)
P.S. I do promise you, my dear Princess Fortuna:
I'll return to marry you sometime quite soon... or sooner.

Without you my humble life is ever incomplete.
More seemly and agreeable a girl I'll never meet.
For company I send you this to while away the hours.
   (Fortuna reveals bird in cage)
It's a token of my love, like cho-co-lates or flowers,
But lasts a good while longer. Like my love it is alive.
Keep it by you as a sign of me 'til I arrive.
Only in the farthest countries can one find this bird.
Such a sweet melodious voice you never will have heard.
It was the favourite of Venturo, whom I have beheaded –
That foul pirate is long gone, no longer to be dreaded.
His dear pet is now a trophy of my brave conquest.
I know you're delighted, and I hope you are impressed.

FORTUNA
Mama! Mama! I have the news we've waited for at last!

(Enter Queen.)

Our days of fear and trembling are firmly in the past.
I've an offer from the Prince – he says he will return.
I've a letter from him, full of fondness and concern,
Promising that sometime soon we shall be man and wife.
Now our country is protected from all future strife.
Look! He sent me this fine bird as proof of his largesse,
And it is a symbol of his soldierly prowess –
He has found Venturo, and has valiantly vanquished!
We are safe, and now my prince will be no longer anguished!
This was the pirate's favourite pet, it is a living prize.
I'm awash with gladness, what a manifold surprise!
How its eyes and feathers shine and sparkle in the sun.
Ah, my dearest playmate, we will have no end of fun!

QUEEN
Oh! I knew that he would fit his heart to our agenda.
I was sure we should not fail and to the south surrender.
Plus that wretched pirate now has met a sticky end.
Alphonse was born to win your heart and our kingdom defend!
You have saved the dignity and pride of this whole land.
This bond will be invincible – no shifty rope of sand.
What a lovely time to marry – just before the spring!
Quickly, right this instant we must go and tell the king,
He'll be cock-a-leekie… I mean he'll be cock-a-hoop!
Not a bad idea though, I'd like a bowl of soup.
Go, I'll catch you up, my feet are killing in these shoes.

(Exit Fortuna.)

Lord, is there no limit to the price we pay for vanity?
This accursed fashion is enough to claim my sanity.

(Exit Queen.)

ACT 1, SCENE 4

(At the palace.)

(Enter Princess Fortuna, kills bird and rips up letters. Enter Queen.)

FORTUNA
Three months have been wasted now, all in this fruitless wait.
Next I dread to wonder what will be our country's fate.
Two-faced and duplicitous, insuff'rable betrayer!
That *un*-dashing Prince I've found is nothing but a player!

He has written rhymes of love to both of the duchesses,
And the meantime his undying troth to *me* professes!
And one poem he has sent to each of us the same.
We are all but pieces in his sordid little game!
Anyway his poetry was utterly appalling,
His letters, like his company, were far short of enthralling.
I heard he can't lift a sword, and is a dreadful coward.
Should have known at once, the way his perfume overpowered.
He didn't fight the pirate and was nowhere near Belize,
He's in *Britain* with no plans to cross the southern seas.
I have heard Venturo is as yet alive and well,
Last seen checking out of some big 5-star French hotel.
Goodness knows where he is plotting his next buccaneering,
Plus we risk invasion now as we had long been fearing.

QUEEN
Oh my dear, have faith, perhaps there is an explanation,
Though of course I understand your anger and frustration.
Maybe he is only shy beneath that brave exterior.
With his... modest... stature he is bound to feel inferior.
Some seem over-confident when they are truly... meek.
Give him one more chance, my dear, for just another week.
Let us see if he returns and if he can explain.
His true nature and intentions we must ascertain.
These scant facts you have revealed need not be quite so
    sinister.
In the meantime I will seek the counsel of Prime Minister.

(Exit Queen.)

FORTUNA *(crying)*
What about the days gone by of honour and nobility?
What are words and wit in lieu of goodness and integrity?
...Invertebrate, unmannerly, unmanly and ham-fisted,

Pompous pom-pom, milksop, chicken-chested and limp-wristed,
Spongy, sissy, cowardy-custard with a heart as yellow
As a... bullfrog's eye... and... and an eye as... Oh, hello!

(Enter Prince Alphonse. Enter Angel, stands behind Fortuna, blesses her and exits.)

PRINCE ALPHONSE
Princess, noble lady, I'll pretend I didn't hear that,
Though it's true: I am quite as bloodthirsty as a fruit bat.
I couldn't fight my way out of an open paper bag,
All I learned in navy school was how to boast and brag.
My favourite sport is playing cards – I'm not too bad at poker –
But exercise just does me in, I'm that much of a smoker.
I can't swim to save my life, how's that for an Admiral?
Jogging in this get-up is an awful rigmarole.
I admit it, I'm a fraud, I'm sorry that I lied.
In coming back at last... at least... I put aside my pride.
Now I mean to see an end to all t'tears you've been shedding.
I promised you I would return and we would have a wedding,
I should say I have a very slightly... different plan,
But you're mature, and I'm quite sure you'll take it like a man.
As a consolation for my spell of impropriety,
I invite you to remain always in my society.
Though... not quite... our wedding, how about a wedding party?
There I fully guarantee the welcome will be hearty.
I have met... another girl, I'll wed her now in spring.
  (Fortuna almost faints)
See, I couldn't help myself, she has me on a string.
I fell hook, line, sinker, and I really lost my head,
So I hope you two will be as sisters now instead.
Truly I meant to return and be your loyal husband,

But I was up in t'Hebrides, and… no man is an island.
There she was all dressed in sacks – been working on
    the farm –
Sling of turnips on her back, four piglets in one arm,
Puffing from a great long pipe, sat on a cask of cider.
Something melted in my heart when I sat down beside her.
At that moment I resolved: who cares about her breeding!
As I have no backbone, that's the woman I've been needing!
Actually… I did already marry her last week.
    (Fortuna almost faints again)
One more lie I told to you, can you believe my cheek?
She already is my Missus, and I am her… Mister.
I will bring her here tomorrow, and she'll be your sister.
    (Fortuna starts to cry, then so does Alphonse)

FORTUNA
Prince Alphonse, I'm sorry I insulted you so gravely.
I shall choose to take this news respectfully and bravely.
I was… distracted… when I found you'd written to my
    cousins,
And you had been courting other ladies… by their dozens,
But I understand it is entirely natural
And logical for an Admiral to admire… all.
My words were unholy, unbefitting a princess.
And I have been far from rational, I must confess.
I tore up your letters, and I slaughtered that poor bird,
If you were in earshot you would possibly have heard.
    (Alphonse nods)
I have been dishonest from the start, it must be said,
I did not love you at all, it was a ploy instead.
I just sought to use you as a shield from invasion,
I was fortunate you needed so little persuasion.
What a clumsy trick, I am so terribly ashamed.
In this awful tragedy I'm really to be blamed.

What is to become of us, we surely cannot tell,
But this is good-bye now, and I truly wish you well.

(Exit Prince Alphonse.)

Mamaaaaaa!

(Exit Fortuna.)

ACT 2, SCENE 1

(At the palace.)

(Enter King, Queen and Prime Minister. Enter Venturo and Fortuna, secretly from different directions. King now holds aside his hair when others speak.)

QUEEN
Minister! Well what a dreadful mess your plan has left!
That bad Prince has snubbed us, poor Fortuna is bereft!
We cannot afford to take your counsel on this matter.
One more two-faced suitor and our daughter's heart may shatter.
We can't rule the country on the back of your caprice,
But we insist that you assist in bringing her true peace!

(Angel enters, blesses King and exits.)

KING
She is such a good girl, she would never hurt a fly…
Though that bird did come off rather badly by and by.
She has spirit, but she is a truly… soulful thing.
In most circumstances so much wisdom does she bring.

Yes, we are in danger from the south still, as you've said –
I am likely to forego my crown if not my head –
But I think it best that we let God be our Defender –
Not unto the south but to the heavens let's surrender.
I say that we give Fortuna a more spiritual life.
How could she be happy as a military wife?
It is plain: to please us was the reason she agreed
To all this Alphonse nonsense. Now God bless us, she is freed.
If we let her live as God intended in His Game,
She is sure to bring us luck and live up to her name.

PRIME MINISTER
Majesties, apologies I humbly submit,
Please proceed to rule this kingdom as you both see fit.
Far too long you've struggled with my mind as your dictator.
Your two gentle hearts combined are infinitely greater.
I have been of service to you forty-seven years,
And I always dreaded it may one day end in tears.
Judge of character has led me to a grave mistake,
He who seemed the hero has admitted he's a fake.
Please allow me one last act of aid in my employment,
Or I'll live out all my days in penitence and torment.

KING
Excellent, I've always known you were a decent chap,
Let's forget our differences, and this awkward mishap.
Say you find a husband now who leads the life monastic.
Most may shun you, though the opportunity's fantastic.
He will have our kingdom – or whatever still remains –
And Fortuna will at last be free from earthly chains.
We have seen monks praying at the river in the morning.
Go and do a reconnoitre while tomorrow's dawning.
See if you can ask them while they're praying by the water

Which of them is willing to be wedded to our daughter.
Any man would love our fair princess to be his bride,
But most saintly people are reluctant to be tied.

(Fortuna comes forward.)

FORTUNA
Mother, Father, I have overheard your conversation,
I always obey your wishes without hesitation.
But to hear you speaking thus has moved my heart to tears.
Your two hearts of love are sure to quell our country's fears.
I have pondered many hours since my sad discovery,
Now my aching heart has found immediate recovery.
Father's right, I cannot find true happiness in status.
My spell of disillusionment came as a cold hiatus –
Heart and head so full of doubts, just like an inner storm –
Now I've reached a turning point, returning to the warm.
I know I must trust my heart now – Father's words are true.
I must marry one who's made of goodness through and through.
I would follow all of your commands without complaint,
But yes, I'd be happiest if I could wed a saint.
I'm too shy to go out and investigate myself,
Minister, please do ensure I'm not left on the shelf.

(Exit Prime Minister, humbly. Exit Venturo, hurriedly.)

QUEEN
Dearest girl, I always knew your outlook was unique.
I can almost see our golden future as you speak.
I first thought your father's plan was far beneath our dignity,
But he's right, in order to create an opportunity
Of finding you a simple man devoted to religion,
We must try to tone down our high-handedness a smidgeon.

Daughter, you will always be our brightest joy and treasure.
Granted, we are batty, but we love you without measure.

(Exeunt.)

ACT 2, SCENE 2

(At the river.)

(Enter monks, followed by Venturo dressed as a monk. Enter Prime Minister.)

PRIME MINISTER
By order of the King and Queen I come here for research,
With a proposition for you good men of the church.
I have come to seek a husband for the fair Princess:
Fortuna the most radiant possessor of finesse,
Graceful elegance, propriety, beneficence.
Whose pure heart is Heaven's rare gem of magnificence…
Plus she is the royal couple's only child and heir –
She'll inherit everything without the need to share.

MONK 1
How *dare* you come and taunt us with your nauseating bargain!
You revolting viper, spouting foul temptatious jargon!
So the Princess needs a husband, and you think we'd care?
Go now from this sacred place or you'll pollute our air!

PRIME MINISTER
Do you *know* who I am, you sack-clothed inconsequence?
I could have you jailed just for your *thoughts* of insolence,
Yet you speak as freely as a fish-wife at her stall.
Seems you do not know how to preserve your life at all.

MONK 2
Nothing you can say or do will coerce me to marry.
On my road to God, a wife is but a rock to carry.
How can I go forward with a yoke around my neck?
Even if the King came here and wrote me a blank cheque,
Even if you say you'll drown me, burn me at the stake,
Deep-fry me in boiling oil, I'll not make the mistake
Of squandering my life on gold or on a woman's beauty.
My vocation is in prayer, and I'll not shirk my duty.

PRIME MINISTER *(to Venturo)*
You seem… different… to the others – you have peace and poise,
While these fellows seek to crush my ears with their noise.
As it seems they have no clear intention to relent,
May I take your silence as a sign that you consent?

(Venturo remains silent.)

MONK 1
Shame, shame, shame! Now he has cast a slur upon us,
He does not defend us while this sinner tries to con us,
Turns up out of nowhere, dressed like one of our good kind –
He didn't much disturb us, so we didn't much mind –
Now he is agreeing to be married with this silence.
What a coward, falling for this rascal's threat of violence,
Turning without question to a life of earthly pleasure,
Living out his days in idle luxury and leisure!

VENTURO
While you strut about like you're the spiritual aristocracy!
I am so disgusted with your heinous hypocrisy.
You're all talk, you reckon you have conquered your desires.
You are not true saints, but filthy counterfeits and liars.

Outwardly you say you have no care for earthly life –
That you'd rather be deep-fried in oil than have a wife –
But inwardly you crave a life of opulence and pleasure.
Your impurities are far too plentiful to measure.
I may not be perfect, but at least I am sincere,
In writing off the outer life I'm not so cavalier.
I have not transcended yet the outer earthly senses,
But I cannot overcome them merely by pretences.
   (to Prime Minister:)
I will marry her, and sooner realise the Supreme,
Than these two-faced fellows merely living in a dream.
I will transcend my desires slowly, one by one.
Rather than pretending all my inner work is done.

PRIME MINISTER
Excellent! At last I found a level-headed saint.
The Princess and your worthy self, I shall at once acquaint!

(Exit Prime Minister.)

MONK 2
Well I never. Such discourtesy is a disgrace!
Brother, come, we've heard enough, we have to leave this place.
That pretender is beneath us. Marriage is frustration,
Frustration is destruction, but we want illumination!
We must dedicate our lives to prayer to win delight.
He is quite deluded, I am sure our way is right!

(Exit Monks. Venturo paces up and down, anguished. Enter Angel blessing him, he then stands with hands folded and head bowed in prayer. Enter Prime Minister and Fortuna.)

PRIME MINISTER
I have brought the Princess to you, as I said I would.

Won't you let her see your face? Do please remove your hood.

(Venturo removes hood, then removes robe altogether to reveal pirate clothes.)

VENTURO
Minister, I must confess that I have changed my mind.
I know she is beautiful, courageous and refined,
And she will inherit quantities of earthly wealth.
I thought I would care for her in sickness and in health.
In a twinkling I thought I'd bestow on her my heart,
And spend my life beside her until death would make us part.
But I'm not a monk, I am a thieving buccaneer –
Nowhere near as saintly as my robes made me appear.
I'm Venturo, bravest and the fastest with a sword,
Strongest and the smartest, but I can't take this reward.
I'd defend this country just depending on my wit
And p'raps a hundred soldiers... but I cheated, I admit.
I overheard the King when his idea was devised,
So I ran ahead of you, but heavily disguised.
Truly it was money that encouraged me to do it,
But how can money be enough? Just as you left, I knew it.
I can have the Princess and her wealth by telling lies,
But if I pray sincerely – not just in a monk's disguise –
I'll attain the highest Truth. Real happiness will follow.
Wealth that's gained by trickery is tenuous and hollow.
She is beautiful, but she is blossoming in youth.
God's Attraction is immortal – it is born of Truth.
I've plundered and I've pillaged and I've looted here and there,
But from today I dedicate my life to Truth and prayer.

(Enter Angel.)

ANGEL *(to Venturo)*

My son, I am pleased with your conviction and sincerity,
But allow me to augment your notion of prosperity.
Marry her you must, but you will still discover Truth.
Your past is behind you, it was greedy and uncouth.
I am happy that your days of thievery are gone,
I am giving you the wealth of Spirit from now on.
This you must combine with money-power to succeed.
Your life's inner cry has reached the highest height indeed.
You have inner light now, and your life is truly blessed,
But you need the outer wealth to make it manifest.
Use this wealth to serve the Truth that now abides inside you.
Heed my words and trust in me, have faith that I will guide you.
  (to both:)
I unite you. From this day you will be man and wife,
Spirit of the inner, matter of the outer life.
  (to Fortuna:)
Daughter, now your husband needs your full and sure assistance.
As one you'll have a happy and harmonious existence.
With him you will realise God much sooner than without.
  (to Venturo:)
With her you will please the Absolute without a doubt.
  (to both:)
The King and Queen are getting old, it soon will be your turn.
Defend the land with courage, kindness, honour and concern.
Realise God and manifest God – God you will fulfil.
In oneness you have every strength, and strength you will instill.
Your land will be safe if you abide by this one principle:
When the inner and the outer join, they are invincible.

(Venturo and Fortuna bow down to Angel.)

6

THE SEEKER-WRITER

BASED ON THE STORY BY SRI CHINMOY:
THE SEEKER-WRITER [23]

CAST
WRITER
LION
TIGER
KING
MINISTER
SOUL
HEART
GOD
COSMIC GOD
SAGE
NARRATOR

First performed in Albufeira, Portugal
December 27th 2013

PROLOGUE

(At Writer's home.)

(Enter Writer.)

NARRATOR
Once there was a seeker who'd developed much sincerity.
By writing books he'd also gained considerable prosperity.
His first one was a comprehensive study of zoology,
Second was a very famous tome on anthropology,
His third was his favourite, it was autobiographical,
Fourth was his most lofty – it was largely theosophical.
Animals, humans, self and God, each subject he'd applauded.
By the greatest in each realm he hoped to be rewarded.

WRITER
Each book I have written, let me go and read aloud
To the best in each field. They will certainly be proud!
My first I will offer to the king of beasts, the lion,
Second to my country's king, the highest human scion.
Third unto the highest in myself I shall address.
Fourth to God, my loftiest is certain to impress!

SCENE 1

(In a forest.)

(Enter Lion.)

WRITER
Lion, lion, your life-force and power all admire!
Your mane so rich, your eyes so deep and wise, yet full of fire!

Poise, grace, speed, oh your deportment is majestic!
Paws so lithe and teeth so bright, your pouncing is elastic!
You are noble, for you only kill when you are hungry.

(Lion roars.)

WRITER
Ah! and so it's written, only roar when you are angry!
How *dare* you roar at me, you rude and most ungrateful beast?
I sing your praise, and what? You want to make of me a feast?

(Exit Lion.)

SCENE 2

(In a palace.)

(Enter King.)

WRITER
Majesty! Your royal highest height of human highness!
This fine work of prose I bring to you, despite my shyness.
In it I explore the farthest reaches of humanity,
And in you I see the depths of goodness, grace and sanity,
So to you I offer my research on human nature.
Your kindness and compassion have this continent in rapture!
Faith and certitude arise in everyone you meet.
Bravery and wisdom just two puppies at your feet.
Blessèd are your people since your pure and noble birth:
In you we see the representative of God on earth.

KING
Thank you.

(Exit King.)

WRITER
Thank you? *Thank* you? Well, my ears must need a clean.
How is it that one so fine and noble speaks so mean?
I offer my own heart in words, all praise and admiration.
"Thank you" is all he can say for such appreciation?
So for nought this life is spent in wordy adoration.
What can a humble writer do when doomed by his vocation,
But weep into the night and seek the solace of his soul.

SCENE 3

(At Writer's home.)

(Enter Soul.)

WRITER
Yes! Let me read my third book, it is sure to reach its goal!
This, my favourite work of prose is all about myself,
I'll not let it sit and gather dust upon a shelf.
Soul, my soul you are the brightest, dearest of possessions,
The purest and the best in me, imparter of great lessons,
To your beauty, this my earthly body is no parallel.
You're the fastest, whitest horse on my life's carousel!
   (Soul smiles)
Fifteen minutes solid, soul, I have admired and praised,
All you do is smile? Well, now I really am amazed!
Of all the aspects of myself I thought you were the best,
But you're much more mean and more ungrateful than rest!

(Soul stops smiling. Exit Soul.)

SCENE 4

(In Heaven.)

WRITER
Wait, my finest literary work I shall reveal!
If not beast or man or soul, then God will surely feel
The meaning of my words – their very depth and clarity.
If none else, then God will see my brilliance and rarity.

(Enter God.)

God, I stand before You now in grateful, warm elation,
Reflecting in amazement at Your vast and grand creation.
Upon Your little Finger-Tip the planets make their dance.
Your Grace is the eye of Time, of Mystery and Chance.
Throughout the universe Your fond Compassion reigns supreme.
I'm glowing with delight to play my part inside Your Dream!

GOD
It is all right.

(Exit God.)

WRITER
All *right*? All *right* only? Woe is me! Alack, alas!
My finest and most lofty work waved off like so much gas?
How could God Himself be so devoid of love and gratitude?
To think I hoped to be like Him! Well I don't like His Attitude!
I hoped at least my Heav'nly Father could say something nice,
But in Him instead I found a heart as hard as ice.
I found only disappointment in so-called superiors,

Let me teach them something – I shall visit their inferiors.
The tiger stands in second place for bravery and might.
I'll choose my words to cunningly assure him of his height.

SCENE 5

(In a forest.)

(Enter Tiger.)

WRITER
Tiger, tiger shining bright, your markings are the oddest,
But in the forest hierarchy, surely you're too modest.
With your skills and courage all the lions you'd defeat!
Such claws, such teeth! You'd mangle any hero into meat!
Lions are just dandies, only strutting, pompous fluff.
All they really do is roar to make themselves look tough!

TIGER
Yes. Yes! I thank you, little human, now I see.
I'm top cat, I *am* all that, it's all about me!

(Writer nods. Tiger struts around, then finds a gold ring on the ground and carries it in his mouth.)

TIGER
What is this? Let's see now, is it something nice to eat?
Yeuch, it's made of gold! What use is anything but meat?

(Drops the ring by the Writer, and exits.)

WRITER
For me? Such a fine, expensive, jewelled, golden ring?

What gratitude the tiger has to give me such a thing!
At last someone has felt my love. My efforts were worthwhile!
So much more one ring is worth than just one measly smile!
With pride and joy abundant now I'll carry on my quest!
One realm loves me, I shall seek the praises of the rest.
If the tiger loves, then let the dumb lion abhor me.
And if not the King, then let his minister adore me.

SCENE 6

(In a palace.)

(Enter Minister.)

WRITER
Minister, you see how you are greater than the King?
Your humility is greatness, I'm not flattering!
Your selfless life in service to your country will pay off,
Every pauper, every lord to you their cap will doff.
With your virtues, wait and see, in time you'll take the throne.
All the riches of this realm are sure to be your own!
You do all the work, and still the King gets all the glory,
But wait and see, in time it's sure to be a different story.

(Minister looks around, gives Writer a big bag of money, then exits.)

A thousand rupees! I was right, and look, here is the proof!
The so-called highest do not know and do not care for truth.
Those below them really see the wisdom of my mind.
In spiritual height I see they leave superiors behind.

SCENE 7

(At Writer's home.)

(Enter Heart.)

WRITER
Heart, my heart, you are so nice, to everyone so kind.
They say the soul's the highest, strongest, deepest, most refined,
But where is that fickle rogue? You're here for all to see.
Your love always offers shelter like a generous tree.
Even doctors know you, and I feel you with each breath.
When you stop, I cannot live, and follow you to death.

(Heart starts to cry.)

HEART
No and never! Words like that come only from a fool.
Have you not learned the ABCs yet at your inner school?
I could never match the divine beauty of the soul.
I am simple as a child, and earthly is my role,
I am honoured all my earthly life the soul to serve.
Praise for higher virtues, no, I never shall deserve.

(Exit heart, crying.)

WRITER
In passing on my lavish praise the heart was oh so hasty,
All to my soul – ungrateful, undivine and oh so nasty!
How my heart is melting at my own sweet heart's humility.
The heart's the greatest part of me, the source of all nobility.

SCENE 8

(In Heaven.)

(Enter Cosmic God.)

WRITER
Cosmic god, I come to offer you all my devotion.
Seems that God is empty of all Fatherly emotion.
I spent my life serving Him with every breath of mine.
"It is all right," He said. How very cold and undivine!
God does nothing well! I made of Him a lovely fuss,
Did He even thank me? No! How can the world be thus?
"All wrong," I now say. My praise was lofty and immense.
I think He's grown old, and is no longer speaking sense.
Your beauty and your wisdom are remarkably superior.
You needn't be suspicious that my motives are ulterior;
I see in you the future God, and offer my obeisance.
I bow to you. In you I hail divinity's renaissance.
I place the flower at your feet that God did not deserve.
In my undying service, I shall love without reserve.

(Places flower at the feet of Cosmic God.)

COSMIC GOD
Idiot! Get out with your foul words to the Supreme!
I wouldn't want to be in your shoes when He lets off steam!
How can you appreciate the love He has for all
With such a craven attitude and with a mind so small?
Fool! You think that I deserve this kind of fancy thing?
He's the Lord, the ultimate and universal King.

(Enter God. Cosmic God places flower at God's Feet.)

Supreme, I bow to Thee, to Thee, Supreme I bow and bow.

(Exit God and Cosmic God.)

WRITER
Respect, I say, and say again, if not before then now!
All of my devotion for himself he could have kept,
But he gave it all to God, I swear I could have wept!
Now I know for certain that the highest are inferior,
And the so-called greatest aren't in any way superior!
In so many ways I put my theory to the test.
Now I think it's time for me to take a well-earned rest.

SCENE 9

(At Writer's home.)

(Writer lies down to sleep. Enter Saint.)

WRITER
What? A dream? Are you a saint or do my eyes deceive me?

SAINT
A vision and a saint I am, I hoped you would receive me.
You're a fool. Your silly theories only tricked your mind.
You tried to seek the highest, but you left the truth behind.
God sent me to teach you, and with some exasperation.
When the lion roared it was with joy and inspiration!
It was his way of thanking you, and showing you he'd heard.
Did you think he'd dance a jig, or twitter like a bird?
What of the King? You think he likes verbose appreciation?
He thanked you, and you only felt a vehement indignation.
He hears praise from many who are greater, more refined,

Less long-winded than you are. To thank you was most kind!
You were lucky that he let you ramble on at will.
From him a nod is praise indeed – a "thank you", greater still!
From your soul you think a smile is such a common thing?
Did you hope to see it jump for joy or start to sing?
Your soul is God on earth, its very smile is His Divinity!
To know that you have pleased your soul is to receive Infinity!
Which reminds me, there is one more thing I have to say.
'It is all right' means that you are right in every way.
God said to your face your words were nothing but perfection.
You became disgusted, but you missed His true Inflection.
For God to give such praise means all your words are ratified!
More than you deserved, but still you were dissatisfied.
Only fools would ever choose self-pity over glory.
Your call though, it's your life and your progress. End of story.
The highest are the highest still, but those who won't believe
Are missing out on blessings they could easily receive.
If we're earnest, pure in faith, and true unto the soul
We may let the greatest lead us to the highest Goal.

7
WE NEED MONEY-POWER TO LIVE ON EARTH

BASED ON THE STORY BY SRI CHINMOY:
WE NEED MONEY-POWER TO LIVE ON EARTH [24]

CAST

HUSBAND 1
HUSBAND 2
WIFE 1
WIFE 2
DOCTOR 1
DOCTOR 2

First performed in Dubrovnik, Croatia
January 11th 2015

SCENE 1

(On a street.)

(Enter Husbands.)

HUSBAND 1
Dearest friend, it must be twenty years since last we met!
So much time has passed, yet here's a face I'd not forget!
In fact I must confess it comes to me as some surprise
To see you so unchanged. Is it the failing of my eyes?
No, indeed up close I clearly see it is the truth.
What's your secret? Tell me, how have you retained your youth?
How'd you come to keep yourself so vigorous and strong?

HUSBAND 2
Friend, I'm glad to see you back, it has been far too long!
Yes I have a secret, let me give you the whole tale
Of how I have remained through age so hearty and so hale.
Truth be told, at first I suffered long through nineteen years.
These twelve months have been a breeze since I have switched careers!
Amongst my many ventures great, a café was the first,
Where customers could while away their hunger and their thirst
At tables on a terrace, soaking up the midday sun,
Or in gentle evenings when their working day was done.
But of course I never had the heart to charge enough,
No I was too soft – to turn a profit turned out tough.
So within a year I'm sad to say that business failed.
I defaulted on my taxes, and was nearly jailed.
Then I came into a little money from an aunt,
And set about applying to the council for a grant.

I opened up that very year a trendy art gallery.
I was sure I'd draw the crowds and then a big salary.
Soon I realised my mistake in choosing the location –
Half a mile from any road, and four miles from a station.
So in very little time another dream had folded.
You should have heard my wife by then! Oh how she raged and scolded.
She had no time for what she called my castles in the air.
That was just my second chance, I hardly thought it fair!
Another *thirteen* businesses of mine would bite the dust.
But here comes the secret as to how I'm so robust:
I let go my ambitions of attaining earthly wealth.
Now you see the good results reflected in my health.
I've renounced it all, and have no need to strike it rich.
I can't say what brought the change, I simply lost the itch.
Who wants to wither out his days weighed down by gems and gold?
Such responsibility would make a young man old.
Who needs to own a yacht or have a name at the casino?
Who wants a brand new sports car from the showroom? Oh, not me, no.
I have watched in wonder as my own desires decrease,
Growing in their stead a bright new happiness and peace.
I'm turning my attention to a quiet, simple life.

HUSBAND 1
I am with you brother, but if only were my wife!
You're a fine example of your spiritual ideal,
But I know exactly how my other half would feel.
How I wish that I could be as practical as you,
Then I would be happy, carefree, therefore healthy too.
Yet, alas, I know she will not take the same position.
She has her mind on other goals. A woman of ambition,
Never satisfied, she always wants a higher rank,

A shrewd and watchful eye on how much money's in the bank.
I work my fingers to the bone, I toil away all hours,
I'm certain that convincing her is far beyond my powers.

HUSBAND 2
Oh, I hear you brother, as I share this very plight!
My own wife as well as yours has failed to see the light.
She's got her own business now, and hopes to make a mint.
No, she'll never understand the perks of being skint.
I forget now what it was she said she plans to sell…
Dresses, handbags, chocolate? Oh, who knows and who can tell?
It's all the same to me of course, this giddy women's stuff.
But one thing is certain: you and I have had enough!

HUSBAND 1
So have countless others like us, since the fall of man!
But now listen brother as I have a cunning plan:
Let the women work together in their shared pursuit,
Sell whatever's sweet or fragrant, delicate or cute,
Make a fortune doing it if that is what they need.
You and I forever from our bondage will be freed:
We'll spend our days in quiet leisure, deep inside the woods,
Far beyond the cares and woes of all our worldly goods!

HUSBAND 2
Brother you are right, of course, our problems will be solved!
It is not their fault they can't be spiritually evolved.
Let us leave them to their life of working and of wishing.
We can build a hut from logs and spend our mornings fishing,
So with little effort we will have our food and shelter,
While the women chase after their fortune helter-skelter.
Let us go and give them just an outline of the news,
Then grab a bite and slope off to the garden for a snooze.

SCENE 2

(At a house.)

(Enter Wives.)

HUSBAND 1 *(to Wife 1)*
Dear, my friend and I have found an excellent solution
To the parting of our ways in terms of… evolution.
We'll go to the forest, you can keep the car and house.
From this day, you need no longer think of me as spouse.

HUSBAND 2 *(to Wife 2)*
Dear, it seems the crux of it has already been said.
Bye then, don't forget to put the cat out before bed.

(Exit Husbands.)

WIFE 1
Just like that they change their minds, and yet they call us fickle?
Just like that they walk away and leave us in a pickle?

WIFE 2
Sister, I confess it comes to me as some relief!
My man and his harebrained schemes have gone beyond belief.
First he tried to make the world into his own possession,
Then doing nothing, earning nothing, soon was an obsession.
I have wondered night and day how we could make ends meet,
I resolved the time is past for taking a backseat.
I'm tired of going hungry, never mind his lofty goals,
My clothes are full of patches and my shoes are full of holes.
I'd already decided I can't take it anymore,
I just wish I'd realised my folly long before.

But now at least, I tell you, I am growing more astute:
I believe the future is in… vegetables and fruit!
Many people nowadays are looking to the diet
For causes of diseases, I've researched it on the quiet.
There's a profit to be made in salads and fresh juices.
The simple reason is that many people make excuses:
Having little time for washing, peeling, grating, chopping,
Adding yet more tins and packets to their weekly shopping.
So last month I went to meet the farmers down the lane.
In the very little time it took me to explain,
They'd given me their blessing and the use of an old truck,
Plus the pick of their own goods, can you believe my luck?
See, it saves them time and effort driving things to market,
Next door even have a spare garage where I can park it.
So around the village I deliver door-to-door,
Vegetables and fruits, salads freshly made, and more.
But, my friend, I'm certain: this is just the very start.
It's a winning formula, I know it in my heart!
It's hard work, I won't deny, but how it brings me joy
To be of use, and all of my capacities employ
For good purpose every day – a reason for my labours:
To pay the bills, and also be of service to my neighbours.
Say you'll join me, sister? I have more work than I need.
Can you see we have not been abandoned – we are freed!

WIFE 1
Yes, my friend, I'll join you, and I thank you for the chance,
Now that both our husbands have led us a merry dance!
Mine was not so wealthy as he'd like to have you think.
Little wonder that he'd turn and leave it in a blink.
He says he works, but actually he's decadent and lazy.
All our early hopes and dreams were starting to grow hazy –
The house is mortgaged to the hilt, the car is hire-purchase.
As for making ends meet, I have done my own researches.

Recently my money worries also have been mounting,
So I went to evening school and studied cost accounting,
Book keeping and many other services financial.
Everything I learned in detail – thorough and substantial –
And this new-found knowledge certainly relieved my tensions.
Just for fun I learned about indemnities and pensions,
Then of course remembered the predicament at hand.
What's the point in thinking of a future safe and grand,
When here and now there are so very many bills to pay?
All the answers to my prayers it seems have come today.
What if I can tell between a bond and a debenture?
Little good it does me without starting a new venture.
Sister, it does look as though our darkest hour has ended.
I believe we can create between us something splendid!

(Exit Wives.)

NARRATOR
So it happened that the men and women parted ways,
And were very satisfied with how they spent their days:
Men in simple peacefulness, released from worldly cares,
Women tired but happy in the selling of their wares.

(Enter Wives with older and happier masks.)

So it was for many years, that is at least until…

SCENE 3

(In the woods.)

(Enter Husbands with older and unhealthier masks.)

HUSBAND 2
Brother, I do not believe I've ever felt so ill.
Every passing mosquito just bites me as it pleases.
I suppose the bugs out here are riddled with diseases –
I'm burning with a fever, yet I shiver with a chill.
Every day is worse, I'm going rapidly downhill.
Every joint is aching and my head is in a vice.
I can't find any comfort… and it isn't very nice.

HUSBAND 1
Brother, I believe our lifestyle starts to take its toll.
Once I used to hanker for a life without a goal.
For a time it seemed idyllic moving slow and lazy,
But I have a feeling it's just served to drive me crazy.
First I spoke in riddles and I didn't bother shaving,
Then I thought I was a goat – that's positively raving.
Now I barely know my name, I only sit and stare.

HUSBAND 2
Yes, my friend, between us we are quite a sorry pair.
I believe the hospital's about a mile away,
Let us start our journey now on foot without delay.

(Exit Husbands.)

SCENE 4

(At a hospital.)

(Enter Doctors. Enter Husbands.)

DOCTOR 1
Sirs, you cannot wander in here of your own accord,
First we need to see some proof that you are both insured,
Or have you sufficient funds to cover all our fees?
Contrary to legend, money doesn't grow on trees.
I would guess you're vagrants and have nothing on your person.

HUSBAND 1
Help us please, I beg you, for our symptoms only worsen.
As you rightly guessed, we two are penniless and poor.
Won't you listen first, instead of showing us the door?

DOCTOR 2
Do you think you're living in a world of milk and honey?
We are busy people here, and frankly time is money,
Hence we must abide by all the rules and regulations.
Family may pay the bills though, have you no relations?

HUSBAND 2
Yes, we have, I mean... we sort of... used to... have our wives,
But I fear they'd chase us off their property with knives.
Long ago, all people and possessions we renounced,
So you see it's... awkward... if we turn up unannounced.
All we wanted was a simple life – just to be happy.

DOCTOR 1
All right, let us talk to them. We'd better make it snappy –
You two both need treatment and you clearly need it fast,

Or in such a desperate state who knows how long you'll last.
I can't really blame you two for seeking an escape
From all your worldly bondage, but it's left you in bad shape!

(Exit Husbands, Enter Wives.)

WIFE 2
No, why should we help them? They are scallywags and fools!
They wandered off and left us there to toil away like mules,
Paying off the mortgage and a mountain of their debts.
Too bad if they changed their minds, we now have no regrets.

DOCTOR 2
Madam, I can understand, but now your husbands suffer.
Their decisions left them both without financial buffer.
They need urgent care now, and we need your help to treat them.
Their conditions worsen, and such ailments could beat them.
Come with us, we really would encourage you to visit,
Just to see them for yourselves. That's not a big ask, is it?

WIFE 1
Fine, then let us see them, but it will not change my mind.
Based on past experience, I'm quite far from inclined
To bail them out of hardship they have brought on their own heads,
But let's pay a visit if they *are* on their deathbeds.

WIFE 2
Sister, I am thinking time has passed, we have no quarrel.
To leave a husband dying there is… probably immoral.
I might change my mind again when I yet see his face,
But let's see, I'll take along a credit card in case.

(Enter Husbands, Exit Doctors.)

WIFE 1
Fools! Who wanted you to strike it very, very rich?
Just we didn't want to end up living in a ditch!
And... to have a few nice things, you know how I love shoes...
It's not as though I wanted you to take me on a cruise.
It was... *mostly* in your heads – you had the wrong impression.
What's so bad in seeking a respectable profession –
Just enough to pay the bills, a simple occupation,
P'rhaps a little in the bank to guard against inflation?

WIFE 2
You decided that the time had come to turn a page,
You believed too long we had you living in a cage.
Now where has your freedom led you? Do you call this peace?
Who'd have thought we'd come to save you? Wonders never cease.
We admit, initially we were a little greedy,
But we couldn't stand to end up with the poor and needy.
We had no idea just how hard we'd end up working,
Partly to pay back the debts accrued by all your shirking.
Yes it's fair to say we had not done our share before,
But that claim is certainly not valid anymore.

WIFE 1
We've all learnt our lessons now, each one has since matured.
Let us pay the doctors, and in time you will be cured.

(Exeunt.)

EPILOGUE

(At a house.)

(Enter Husbands, back in their healthy masks. Enter Wives.)

NARRATOR
Soon the husbands were released to their respective spouses,
Then to live a normal life in two adjoining houses.
All four shared the work of selling vegetables and fruit,
So they each could put behind a very long dispute.
We need money-power so that we can live on earth,
But giving it too much attention takes away life's worth.

8
LAOSEN DOES THE IMPOSSIBLE

BASED ON THE STORY BY SRI CHINMOY:
LAOSEN DOES THE IMPOSSIBLE [25]

CAST
SUN GOD
KARNASEN (A FORMER KING)
KING GAUR
RANJABATI (KING GAUR'S SISTER-IN-LAW)
KRIPAN (KING GAUR'S BROTHER-IN-LAW)
LAOSEN

First performed in Kalamata, Greece
January 1ˢᵗ 2017

SCENE 1

(Enter Sun God from east, exit west. Enter Karnasen.)

KARNASEN
I am Karnasen, although perhaps you doubt my word.
This figure may not tally with the stories you have heard
From years long past, now lost within the annals of my youth.
Yes, I'm Karnasen, it has turned out a heavy truth.
I carry only dreams of all the battles I have scored,
And riches I collected then by way of my reward.
Lightning quick, they used to say, and stronger than a horse.
   (laughs modestly)
Good and just, I hope at least – I never ruled by force.
That last war, though fairly fought, came at tremendous cost.
My childhood bride, my warrior sons, my palaces were lost.
My armies then were slaughtered – every animal and man.
Call it luck or call it fate, this new life then began.
My enemy soon let me free, and sent me on my way.
"Go, good king," he gently said, "your hair is fading grey,
Your day is done, your time is past, go peacefully and rest."
Through his honour and compassion I knew I was blessed,
Yet wandered here with nothing but the clothes upon my back,
Peering at a future I saw miserable and black.
I slept in forests on the way – what else can outcasts do? –
Till I was offered shelter and the kindest welcome too.
My rooms are bright, the air is sweet, the grounds are like no other.

(Enter Gaur.)

King Gaur it was who took me in, as would a long-lost brother.
I want for nothing – I have been bestowed a second life.

GAUR
Nothing? Are you certain? What about a second wife?

KARNASEN
Wife! Then what, a family? At my decrepit age?
My heart is weak, my eyes are dull, how would I earn a wage?
   (laughs ironically)
I take comfort in my peace – to marry would be madness.

GAUR
Your defeat has worn you down – you are but aged by sadness.
A wife will do the power of good, her company will cheer you.
And can you doubt the joy of having little children near you,
To play and sport and learn from you all that your days have known –
Legends of your valour and the empires you have grown?
Teach them all the skill you earned, and raise them even stronger!
Do it now, I urge you not to leave it any longer. *(laughs cheekily)*
I have one in mind – the youngest sister of the Queen –
Sweet of nature, and the fairest face you will have seen.
Calm of bearing too – she will not rob you of your peace.
I promise you, your happiness then cannot but increase.
Must you stretch out all your days in quietude and sorrow?
Ranjabati is her name, I'll send for her tomorrow,
Then I'll introduce you, if you *kindly* would allow.

KARNASEN
Will *she* like *me*?

GAUR
Yes... Oh must I list *your* virtues now?

(Exit both, laughing.)

SCENE 2

(Enter Sun God from east, exit west. Enter Kripan.)

KRIPAN
I am Kripan, as you know, world famous… in these parts:
Brave, cunning, clever and proficient in dark arts.
Second to the throne am I, that is but one credential.
Gaur's only son died in his sleep…
   (laughs guiltily)
…so I have great potential.
But I'm *parched* with bitterness, I cannot bear the shame –
My sister Ranjabati has brought down my family name.
I was at war… or something of that nature I am certain,
When Karnasen, that devious brute, crept from behind the curtain,
Took my sister for his bride, with none of my permission!
He is nothing but a beggar, with a fool's ambition.
My sister is a failure, her honour is defiled:
Two years since she married him and yet she has no child!
It was Gaur's grave error letting Karnasen in here.
My hackles rise whenever that foul parasite is near.
He wormed his way into our world and wants to overturn it.
There is some conspiracy, though I cannot discern it.
I hear the two men laughing, and their secrecy is sworn.
Some nights they forego their sleep, and talk until the dawn.
They ride together side by side, shoot arrows and play chess.
That ought to be my privilege – this is a rotten mess!
I must have what is my due – my fate is far from sealed.

(Enter Ranjabati.)

(to Ranjabati:)
You're a useless woman, you are but a barren field!

(Exit Kripan, Ranjabati starts to cry, enter Karnasen.)

KARNASEN
Ranjabati! Come now, tell me what has happened here.
Never since I met you have I seen you shed a tear.
What on earth could shake your poise and bring so much
    distress?

RANJABATI
Shame and sadness both, and such that words cannot express!
A woman of good character I ever long to be,
Yet that self I cannot reach – a stranger still is she.

KARNASEN
Unparalleled your character, and rich with every virtue!
People judge and criticise – you never let it hurt you,
But until you bear a child, you will not feel complete.

RANJABATI
I'll go to the Sun God now and place this at his feet.
I know the chants and rites and I perform them every day,
But I must set aside my life and most sincerely pray.
'Til I know he's heard me, I shall fast and forego sleep.
I must leave at once, for I have promises to keep.

KARNASEN
Godspeed, dearest, I believe your answer is secure.
How can gods ignore petitions from a heart so pure?

(Exit Karnasen. Enter Sun God from east, exits west, Ranjabati follows with folded hands.)

SCENE 3

(Enter Laosen, running.)

LAOSEN
You don't know me yet, hello, they call me Laosen –
My mother Ranjabati and my father Karnasen.
I've not much to tell you as I am but seventeen,
I've not cut my teeth on life, but am keyed up and keen!

(Exit Laosen, running. Enter Karnasen and Gaur behind.)

GAUR
Ah, your boy! Where does he get his energy and strength?
Every day it seems he covers half the country's length!
Right from childhood he was drawn to wrestle and to fight,
Yet he's charming, sweet of nature, ever a delight.
You have raised him well, the boy must ever do you proud.

KARNASEN
Yes, he does so every day – by nothing is he cowed.
He fights with tigers and with whales – the boy is in his prime!
Three or four grown men you know he takes on at a time.
But I take no credit for the way he has turned out.
He's the Sun God's gift to us – of that I have no doubt.
He is a phenomenon, a miracle, a boon.
To all things born of darkness it appears he is immune.
Had not Ranjabati made her solitary prayer,
We would not be fortunate to have him in our care.

GAUR *(looking behind)*
Ah, now here comes Kripan, he is constantly suspicious,
The atmosphere around him is distinctly inauspicious.
Though he's of this kingdom, does he seek to overturn it?
There is some conspiracy, though I cannot discern it.

(Exit Gaur and Karnasen. Enter Kripan from behind.)

KRIPAN
Why ever did I taunt my sister? Then from worse to worse!
Since Laosen was born he's borne me nothing but a curse.
Gaur adored him from a babe – how he would coo and dandle.
To watch him grow into a man is more than I can handle.
He sickens me – his frame so light, yet stronger than an ox.
He fights so fair, and thinks so fast, so tiresome to outfox.
How they praise and cheer him on, and never will desist –
Laosen this and Laosen that – so do I not exist?
I have royal blood and I am second to the throne,
Yet these beggars take my place – it riles me to the bone.
Rage it boils within me such that I can barely function.
Kill Laosen? Oh if I could, I would have no compunction!
But *how*, I ask? How many times have I found new ideas,
Only to be thwarted – there is nothing that he fears.
Once I hired ruffians to stab him in his bed,
He just got a minor cut that hardly even bled.
Once I gave a banquet 'in his honour' at my palace,
My idea went awry – that was a poisoned chalice.
So I sent mad elephants to chase him home at night,
But he saw it as a game and laughed while taking flight!
This has gone on long enough, we cannot coexist.
I shall make the King a threat that he cannot resist.

(Enter Gaur.)

(to Gaur:)
Banish Laosen from this place, King Gaur, I entreat you!
If not, I shall leave and raise an army to defeat you!

GAUR
Kripan, are you ill? What has inflamed this fit of rage?
Let us calmly talk this through, your anger to assuage.

How could I consider banishing a dear relation?
And why should I do it when there is no accusation?
If he goes, he leaves us with the odds against us stacked –
Who would then defend us if our kingdom is attacked?
He's our secret weapon – no opponent can defeat him.

KRIPAN
Really? Is he such a *god* that mortals cannot beat him?
Will he do what's impossible, this darling boy of yours?
I speak of things beyond the mere art of waging wars.

GAUR
Impossible? He does not know the meaning of the word.

KRIPAN
Really? I will show you that your statement is absurd.
I will take your word for it but on one sole condition –
This one feat, and this alone will bow me to contrition –
Can Laosen the hero make the sun rise in the west?

GAUR *(pauses to think)*
I am certain you will even see him pass that test.

(Exit Gaur.)

KRIPAN
Ah, what sport will follow on the folly of the king!
Blinded by his love… and love does have a nasty sting.
Sunrise in the west? Oh I will come and watch that show.
Pigs will fly, presumably, and hell will have some snow.

(Exit Kripan.)

SCENE 4

(Enter Laosen, running, looking. Enter Gaur, tentatively.)

LAOSEN
Do not worry, good King Gaur, your promise I have heard.
I cannot see how just yet, but I shall keep your word.
Mother asked the Sun God for my life, thus I was born.
He is my progenitor — I am the child of dawn.
I offer my devotions and I thank him every day,
But I must set aside my life and most sincerely pray.
'Til I know he's heard me, I shall fast and forego sleep.
I must leave at once, for we have promises to keep.

(Exit Laosen to the east, running. Exit Gaur, worried. Enter Sun God from the east, Laosen follows with folded hands. They stand beside each other. Enter Kripan and Gaur.)

KRIPAN
Look at this rank fool who thinks the sun will change its course.
Here is one thing he cannot accomplish just by force.
Three days we have waited — clearly it cannot be done.

GAUR
Give him time and he will do it, you have not yet won.

(Exit Kripan and Gaur.)

SUN GOD
Laosen, I am pleased with you, O child of my light.
I will try to grant your wish, but heavy grows the night.
I must leave your company, come back to me at morn.
Carry on your prayer meanwhile, as sleep you have forsworn.

(Exit Sun God to west. Laosen follows, then returns.)

LAOSEN
He will try, but gods are not aware of earthly time.
Uncle is impatient and is predisposed to crime.
I must preserve the honour and the safety of the king,
But for the sun to change its course is not a trifling thing.
I must find a way to show him I am most sincere –
That I truly am his child and have transcended fear.
The ultimate in sacrifice is difficult indeed,
But it is the only way in time I might succeed. *(pauses)*
I shall cut off my own head to show him my devotion.
Words have strength, but deeds contain the power of an ocean.
If I merely die, I know that I have done my best,
But if my gesture pleases, let the sun rise in the west.

(Exit Laosen east. Sound of a sword. Enter Sun God from east, holding Laosen's head.)

SUN GOD
All now hail, and look upon the face of true devotion!
Yea, for this would all the stars and gods adjust their motion.
If you say I'm bound by my predictable condition,
I will answer: you are right, I am no great magician.
I'll not change my course for entertainment or for threats,
Or because some braggart has decided to place bets.
If Kripan had come to me and challenged me directly,
I would still be navigating through the sky correctly,
But what will I not do for my sincere devotee?
Myself perhaps you can defeat, but surely never he.
God has never any need to prove He is Supreme,
And knows impossibility is but a human dream.
For devotees, impossibility does not exist,
As God Himself will change the course of nature to assist.

Never challenge devotees, for you will surely lose.
  (to Laosen's head:)
Now you must away and tell your family the news!
  (Pauses teasingly, then continues, laughing fondly)
Come, Laosen, I will undo the workings of your knife.
You have pleased me such that I will give you back your life.
Kripan, for his cruelty, I have devised a curse:
Leprosy. You see in his case nothing could be worse.
To you a life in exile was the fate he tried to deal.
Now comes his opportunity to learn how outcasts feel.

SCENE 5

(Exit Sun God west. Enter Laosen west. Enter Karnasen, Ranjabati and Gaur east, followed by Kripan.)

LAOSEN
Father, Mother and King Gaur, I have tremendous news!
The Sun God now has promised, so we surely cannot lose –
From the west the sun will rise for certain in the morning!
Come, the night has nearly passed, and day will soon be dawning!

KRIPAN
Ah, he specifies a time, I hold him to that word!
In the morning – that is set, and cannot be deferred.
If it does not come to pass, then you must throw him out.

GAUR
Yes, but he will do it, I am not in any doubt.

(They all wait, facing west. Enter Sun God west.)

9
THE GODS GAIN IMMORTALITY

BASED ON THE STORY BY SRI CHINMOY:
THE GODS GAIN IMMORTALITY [26]

CAST
BRIHASPATI (GURU OF THE COSMIC GODS)
SUKARACHARYA (GURU OF THE DEMONS)
COCH (SON OF BRIHASPATI)
DEBAJANI (DAUGHTER OF SUKARACHARYA)
DISCIPLE 1
DISCIPLE 2 (MUTE)

First performed in Budva, Montenegro
December 30th 2017

PROLOGUE

(Enter Brihaspati and Sukaracharya.)

BRIHASPATI
Gods and demons tooth and nail have fought throughout the ages,
Devastation and destruction litter history's pages.
How many aeons even time itself has lost the count.
The problem of this tit-for-tat it seemed none could surmount,
But the embodiment of sacrifice before you stands.
(points to Sukaracharya)
The story of his goodness is renowned in eastern lands.
Guru of the demons, Sukaracharya is his name.
Who could know the crucial part he'd play in this long game?
The gift of life: to this old secret he once held the key.
How might this bring peace amongst our people? You will see.
Though life and all its many complications may enmesh us
Who'll deny the simple fact that life itself is precious?

SUKARACHARYA
Ah, I am an old man now, my friend, you flatter me!
(to audience:)
In wisdom and compassion none can ever equal he:
Brihaspati, you will surely recognise his name,
Guru of the gods! …Though we care not for earthly fame.
Mark my words, there is no measuring his ample virtue.
But once any Guru gives his word, he'll not desert you.
The quality of constancy, yes that at least I'll claim.
I say any real Guru would have done the same
As I did those years ago, if in the same position.

BRIHASPATI
A Guru's love must know no bounds, and come without

condition.
This one truth eternal is essential to our tale.
Listen, and the sequence of events we shall unveil.
Sukaracharya had a mantra to revive the dead,
So, far from them dwindling, the demons thrived instead.
For all my long experience I did not know this chant,
So when the gods implored me for the same, I said, "I can't".
How it riled and pained me to refuse their intercession!
But here I must tell you that I have a small confession.
You have heard the saying: all is fair in war and love –
That rings true on earth, and just so in the worlds above.
Thus despite the demons and the hideous wars they'd wage,
I sent my own son to study with their master sage.
(points to Sukaracharya)
Even amongst enemies a Guru you may choose,
And if the Guru sees you are sincere, need not refuse.
Such happenings are not uncommon in our old tradition.
I digress now, and as promised, here is my admission:
I did not tell my son Coch the secret of my quest.
In fondness and obedience he went at my behest
To learn some wisdom and some use of weapons from our rival.
Little did he know how it would threaten his survival.
There's no limit to the ways in which a Guru serves,
Giving what the student needs… and not what he deserves.
The gods had the idea that I send my dearest boy:
Brilliant scholar, brave of heart, he was my pride and joy.
How could I refuse my spiritual children in their need?
Love it was that drove me to this questionable deed.
With such innocence, and with an eagerness to learn,
Coch left for the lower worlds, p'rhaps never to return.

(Exit Brihaspati.)

SCENE 1

(At the ashram.)

(Enter Disciples.)

SUKARACHARYA
Where has Debajani gone? Today I have not taught her
Any songs, now go away and look! Where is my daughter?
Debajani, come and learn… and bring a little snack.

(Disciple offers food from his pocket. Enter Coch.)

I am pinched with hunger. No, you go and bring her back!
Stupid boys, have you no ears? Be gone, you should be looking!
I eat Debajani's food, you think I trust your cooking?

(Exit Disciples.)

COCH
Master, I have seen her in the dairy, I will fetch her.

SUKARACHARYA
They are gone, at least, so I may spare myself the lecture.
Good boy, Coch, yes go and ask her back, my dearest student.
To trust those oafs with anything important is imprudent.

(Exit Coch.)

My girl Debajani, ah, where would I be without her?
What a scholar, there's a touch of genius about her.
Yet all things she does with simple joy and pure humility.
It would seem to me there are no bounds to her ability.
Coch, though he is of the gods, is similarly matched.

As time goes on I see those two increasingly attached.
It is something more than admiration and affection.
While he's from another world, I would have no objection
To their marrying, when they both reach a certain age,
But I need not broach it now, we're not yet at that stage.
This boy and my daughter both, I love with all my heart,
I can see no reason why they should remain apart.

(Enter Debajani, followed by Coch and Disciples. Disciples point as though to present her, then make to leave, but eavesdrop.)

DEBAJANI
Father, are you hungry? I have brought some honey cake.

SUKARACHARYA
Debajani, come! How do you find the time to bake?
You're a wonder, good girl, yes some honey cake please bring,
Take some too, your voice will sound the sweeter when you sing.
Coch, go to the armoury and sit amongst the spears.
To learn to tame a weapon with your hands will take you years.
Your journey is a long one, and you've barely yet begun
Just hold the weapon, meditate, and with it become one.
Oh, but first go to the well and draw a pail of water,
Take it to my room while I am singing with my daughter.

COCH
Water is already there and waiting for you, Master.

SUKARACHARYA
There, he does it in a flash! Would lightning travel faster?
Blessings to you, Coch, good boy, you are my feet and hands.
You are not just heeding, you're pre-empting my commands!
Hurry or you will not have the time to fetch the cattle.

Later bring me news and stories from the latest battle.

COCH
Master, certainly, for you I only live to serve.

(Exeunt.)

SCENE 2

(At the ashram.)

(Enter Disciples.)

DISCIPLE 1
Ugh! I cannot stand the boy, he really has a nerve.
He thinks he's so special, but he just comes from the *gods*!
Debajani loves him most of all, what are the odds?
Surely it is clear that she should marry demon blood.
No, I cannot bear to see her name dragged through the mud.
Why does Master dote on him and give him such attention?
I can't stand that sneaky little weasel, did I mention?
The gods go on tormenting us, both in and out of season.
Why don't we just kill him? Can you think of any reason?
Tending to the cattle is amongst his many tasks.
Since he always does precisely as the Master asks,
He will be out in the meadow close to five o'clock.
  (Coch enters as though in their imagination)
I will hide some stones and bits of metal in a sock.
Just a sock, so it will seem – no reason to suspect –
Then you'll thrash him on the head when he would least
   expect!

(Disciple 2 thrashes Coch and he lies down. Exit Disciples.)

(Enter Sukaracharya, working. Enter Debajani, running.)

DEBAJANI
Father, please come to the meadow now, we must be quick!
Coch was bludgeoned from behind, it must have been a trick!
I was worried when he missed his time to round the cattle.
(cries softly)

SUKARACHARYA
And I, daughter, when he failed to bring me news of battle.

(Follows to the meadow, where Coch is lying, and inspects the body.)
Left here in the meadow as though he might be forgotten?
Here's the work of dark in darkness, with a motive rotten.
Such a sharp blow to the head nobody could survive.
Give me space and silence while the poor boy I revive.

(Enacts the chant in silence. Coch revives and stands with folded hands, unsteady on his feet.)

COCH
Master, Debajani, I have had the strangest dream!

SUKARACHARYA
Steady, Coch, stand easy, things are not quite as they seem.
While tending to the cattle you sustained a fatal blow.
Who would do this to you, child? That we may never know.
But perhaps you might consider carrying a knife.

COCH
I am gratitude to you for bringing back my life –
Only gratitude, indeed the past for me is dust.
What need have I of self-defence when in your love I trust?
Do you think it possible that somebody has tricked me?

Master, what if it is simply that a cow has kicked me?

SUKARACHARYA
Faith is good, my dear one, yes, but so is common sense.
I appreciate your living in the present tense,
But you're in the lower worlds, where there are no holds barred.
Now come home and rest with us, that death blow... hit you hard.

DEBAJANI
Coch! To have you back with us is worth the highest cost.
Oh, without you in our lives we would be fairly lost.

(Exeunt.)

SCENE 3

(At the ashram.)

(Enter Disciples.)

DISCIPLE 1
Idiot! Of course the Master would just bring him back.
We must try again, but this time tie him in a sack,
Drag him down the sandy bank and throw him in the river.
He sickens me, I tell you, that insufferable self-giver.
Wait, I have a better plan: we down him with a bash,
Like the time before, but then we burn him into ash,
The ash we use to mix with juice and make a special drink,
Then give him to the Master in a cup. What do you think?

(Exit Disciples.)

(Enter Sukaracharya, working. Enter Disciples.)

SUKARACHARYA
What now? Please come quickly, I have many things to do.

DISCIPLE 1
Please excuse us, Master, we have made a drink for you.
We understand why you do not appreciate our cooking,
And perhaps your dearest ones are somewhat better looking.
We're clumsy and incompetent, and we do not deserve you.
Still, we long for any opportunity to serve you,
So we made this special drink of pomegranate juice.

(Sukaracharya beckons and drinks, while still distracted by work. Enter Debajani, running.)

DEBAJANI
Father, stop! Put down the cup, it is a cunning ruse!

(Exit Disciples, running.)

SUKARACHARYA
What is this concoction? It has made me rather queasy.
Debajani
Father, it is little wonder that you feel uneasy,
This is not just pomegranate juice as you might think,
The ashes of your dear boy Coch were added to this drink.
Now that you have drunk it, he is surely gone for good.

SUKARACHARYA
Ah... there's little wonder it did not taste as it should.
It is true: if I revive him, I will surely perish.
I'll not ask if it is Coch or me whom you most cherish.

(Debajani starts crying.)

DEBAJANI
I know I have said that he is worth the highest cost,
But without my Guru, I would be forever lost.

SUKARACHARYA
Come now, my sweet girl, I cannot bear to see you cry.
Come, I am an old man, it is time for me to die.
I've experienced many things – some good, some others bad.
God knows I am thankful for the happy life I've had.
There's no reason to remain in this world any longer.
Debajani, dearest, you must grow a little stronger.
Everybody's time must come, and now I should retire.
Life is but a firefly, this body is but maya –
Flimsy and ephemeral – but this soul is supernal.
I'll never leave you inwardly – my love remains eternal.
With equanimity and courage, please accept this fate.
Leave me to perform the chant, before it is too late.
This will not be easy, but I'm certain he will live.

(Exit Debajani, reluctantly.)

With my blessings, chela, my last breath I gladly give.

(Sukaracharya falls. Coch rises.)

COCH
Master, you have saved me once again from the abyss.
The dust of the dust of your feet do let me kiss.
For my life you gave your own, I never can repay you,
Yet you have my promise: I shall evermore obey you.
To think of how you suffered here is utterly appalling…
But the mantra to revive the dead, I am recalling!

Though my faults and failings are too many to be measured,
If at least I could bring back this life so deeply treasured,
My life and death, life and death again are not in vain.
Please God, I implore you, let my Master live again!

(Coch enacts the chant. Sukaracharya stands.)

SUKARACHARYA
Coch, you saved me with the special mantra you have learned!

COCH
Master, it is by your grace to us you have returned.
That first time you brought me back, the words came in a haze.
The second time I heard them very clearly, phrase by phrase.
Now I see! The first time I was lying down beside you.
This time, as your very being, I was right inside you.

SUKARACHARYA
Blessings to you, dear one, you have learned more than my skill,
And as you'll see, your father's secret wish you will fulfil.
You learned that to make your progress infinitely faster,
You must have inseparable oneness with your Master.

EPILOGUE

(Enter Brihaspati.)

BRIHASPATI
So both Coch and Sukaracharya were in time restored.
Debajani thus regained the father she adored,
But her new rejoicing soon gave way to dawning sadness.
To marry Coch, she realised then, would be a certain madness.

He'd come from her father, so of course that was taboo.
He was now her brother, so their union would not do.
Yet she treasured him no less, because her heart was pure,
A life of simple friendship she would willingly endure.
Coch was loved by Debajani, hence some rogues were jealous –
Were they not, they might not have been quite so over-zealous.
In the history of our worlds, the rascals played their part,
As did Coch in his turn, with his wide and generous heart.
My own son brought back my erstwhile rival from the dead,
But for my son's life, the Guru gave his life instead.
Like a real Master, he has shown his heart's nobility –
Even for his enemy he bore no animosity.
Since then in our different worlds, true peace has reigned supreme.
In the game of life there is not one immortal team,
But two, so all the fighting had to reach a natural end –
There is little point in killing soldiers who will mend.
True, the gods gained immortality by hook or crook,
But for eternal peace we might not do things by the book.
So our story, as you see, begins and ends with love.
Love has the force to move the worlds below, just as above.

10
CONVERSATIONS

BASED ON THE STORIES BY SRI CHINMOY:

THIS PLANT IS MAN, THIS PLANT IS GOD [27]
PLAY YOUR ROLE AS A DAUGHTER OF GOD [28]
TWO DISCIPLES [29]
THE UNCONDITIONAL GIFT [30]
RENUNCIATION IS NOT THE ANSWER [31]
THE SPIRITUAL LESSON [32]
THE FIGHT IS FOR THE BRAVE [33]
CONQUER YOUR ENEMIES [34]
HUMAN EXPECTATION AND DIVINE FULFILMENT [35]
EVERYONE HAS HIS OWN ROLE [36]
THE HEAVIEST LOAD [37]
WHO IS MORE IMPORTANT – GURU OR GOD? [38]
THE TWO FRIENDS [39]

CAST

MASTER
DISCIPLE 1
DISCIPLE 2

First performed in Funchal, Madeira
Act 1, January 7th 2019 – Act 2, January 10th 2019

PROLOGUE

(Enter Master, limping.)

MASTER *(to audience)*
My God, spiritual guidance is relentless, heavy work.
My multifarious duties I would often rather shirk.
P'rhaps I'm blessed, for I have but a single spiritual daughter,
And she takes to heart most of the lessons I have taught her.
In the coming stories you will see how progress flowers.
I shall first bestow upon you certain occult powers.
Concentrate and you will know the art of reading minds.
Hold still and prepare to open all your inner blinds.

(Master makes a flourish.)

ACT 1, SCENE 1

(In the ashram garden.)

(Enter Disciple 1, gardening aside with Master. Enter Disciple 2.)

DISCIPLE 2
Ah, this is a sacred place. Oh, what a peaceful garden.
How they work in harmony... Hello, I beg your pardon!
Sir, you have the look about you of a spiritual Master?
I ask as I would like to realise God... a little faster.
I notice your disciple always seems to do your bidding.

MASTER *(to audience)*
Well if only that were true, I don't know who she's kidding

DISCIPLE 2
Is it possible for her to realise the Supreme
By following your teachings, or is that a girlish dream?
I'm a worldly person and I cannot find a guide,
Though for many years I have been searching far and wide.
Seems it is impossible that such a one exists
Who'll guide a hopeless seeker such as I am through the mists,
Let alone one great enough to take me to the goal.
   (to audience:)
I'm not sure one as bad as me would even have a soul!

MASTER
Others may take sides with you, but I must disagree.
To realise God for anyone is simple as can be.
Now look here, these little plants are rooted in the sod.
Take this plant as you, my child, and this one take as God.
Now I am the Master, I came here and touched this plant.
I have done in moments that which you have said you can't.
This tiny thing immediately responded to my touch.
In the blinking of an eye, this God-Plant as such
Gave me all His Joy, Delight, Compassion and His Love.
I merely switched them, but the act was sanctioned from
    above.

DISCIPLE 2
Master, I have found you, please give me initiation!

MASTER
Soon, my child, but let me first explain your great frustration.
Your ideas of God and spirituality are not right.
When I approach you, you have fear and think of taking flight.
You're ashamed, your ignorance you're eager to conceal,
But this plant has no shyness if its brown roots I reveal.
It rises to adventure, look its very leaves are thrilled!

Offer up your darkness, and your wish may be fulfilled.

(Exit Disciples.)

ACT 1, SCENE 2

(At the ashram.)

(Enter Disciple 2.)

DISCIPLE 2
Master, you may not yet have my heart of true devotion.
It's just that now my life is full of worry and commotion,
But I promise that will not much longer be the case.
My life will soon be marching at a somewhat slower pace.
Now my sons are studying, which is a great distraction.

MASTER
And when they graduate, your mind will meet with satisfaction?
No, they'll work in medicine, in law and in gymnastics,
You think your sons will see the light and turn into monastics?
No, you'll say *then* is the time for finding each a wife,
And believe me, that is the *beginning* of your strife.
There'll be children – three times three or maybe even more.
They'll be scattered far and wide from here to Bangalore,
With studies and professions and more marriages to match.
How do you imagine you will manage to detach?

DISCIPLE 2 *(to audience)*
Drat, he's right of course, I really didn't think this through.
I must try to deceive him, it's the only thing to do.
 (to Master:)

No, just wait a while… until their little ones are grown,
Then I promise, Master, that my life will be my own.

MASTER
Oh yes, very good, so at the age of ninety-nine?

DISCIPLE 2
But it is my duty that I care for all that's mine.

MASTER
It was God who brought you to the life of aspiration.
Call has come! Arise, awake, and seize your inspiration!
With one foot in the grave your days will then be disappearing.
Your boys are men now, do you think they need you interfering?

DISCIPLE 2 *(to audience)*
He is not a mother, so how could he understand?
For my little darlings I would give up my right hand!
They would get so *thin* without my homemade gulab jamun!
Will they live on cupcakes, Bombay mix and instant ramen?
No I'll take them tiffin boxes, like a good relation.
Master will not know… unless I'm late for meditation.

MASTER
Duties are like ocean waves, they never will subside.
To make progress, you must learn to dive against the tide.
The inner life requires that you are focused, steadfast, brave!

DISCIPLE 2
But I'm *limited*, I can't surmount a single wave!

MASTER
You are limited, but not so *my* heart of compassion.

Avail yourself of all I offer… in a timely fashion.
You've played your role as mother, now recall you are God's daughter.
Go to His vast Sea of Love, and plunge into the water.
Leave your sons quite safely in the Lap of God's Concern.

DISCIPLE 2
Master, you are right, I have so very much to learn.

(Exit Disciple 2.)

ACT 1, SCENE 3

(At the ashram.)

(Enter Disciple 1.)

DISCIPLE 1
Master, it grows cold outside, the snow begins to fall.
I have saved on housekeeping to buy you this fine shawl.

(Master accepts shawl. Exit Master. Enter Disciple 2.)

DISCIPLE 2
Look, I told you that the Master has no occult power.
He has *nothing*, it's all lies, my love for him grows sour.
For months now he's been suffering from that rheumatic pain.

DISCIPLE 1
Do we really have to go through all this once again?

DISCIPLE 2
We've done nothing wrong, and yet he says he takes our karma.

He's done something wrong, not us.

DISCIPLE 1
Now will you stop this drama!

DISCIPLE 2
God made two types of people: the deceivers and deceived.
These outlandish claims of his are not to be believed.
Stay with him and suffer with him, with him you will die.

DISCIPLE 1
I'd die with him, and for him gladly.

DISCIPLE 2
Fine for you, not I.

(Enter Master.)

MASTER *(to Disciple 2)*
So you think my sacrifice for you is only bragging?
Go then, leave me, I will travel faster without dragging
Some ungrateful weight behind me. I have better things to do.
   (to Disciple 1:)
You believe all I have said on suffering is true?
Is it mental knowledge you have gathered just from books,
Or do you really *feel* my pain is deeper than it looks?

DISCIPLE 1
Master, I am sure of what you take from me each day:
Impurity, obscurity, you gently wash away,
Insecurity and jealousy and pride and doubt,
Many other imperfections you are clearing out.

MASTER
Where do they go?

DISCIPLE 1
I give them to you – daily I observe it.
You take them in secrecy, though I may not deserve it.

MASTER
Child, there are two reasons why I suffer in this way.
One is that I bear the ignorance you give away.
In secrecy I do it, yes, this is what God expects.
It's the quickest way, but it has physical effects.
The other is that people sometimes come with their desire –
Not true aspiration – so I cannot take them higher.
They come to me and see that I am paralysed with pain.
They're doubtful, disappointed, and they don't come back again.
God *wants* these unaspiring people to release their Master.
His boat is lighter then, you see, so he may travel faster.
He is left with true disciples, faithful and sincere.
These disciples know and feel their role in life is clear:
Just to give their Master joy, and please him in his way.
To make the Master proud, and prouder of them every day.

DISCIPLE 2
Master, for so long I've been a cruel and faithless creature.
Now I know you are my dearest friend and only teacher.

DISCIPLE 1
Master, I have followed you thus far with my devotion.
Now you have revealed to me your vast compassion ocean,
I feel myself a conscious part of you – a leg or arm.
May this oneness help to keep you physically from harm.

MASTER
By truly understanding what my sacrifice is worth,
You have manifested the Supreme's Will here on earth.

(Exit Disciple 2.)

ACT 1, SCENE 4

(At the ashram.)

DISCIPLE 1
Master, what has happened to that shawl of fine angora?

MASTER
I gave it to a gentleman significantly poorer.

DISCIPLE 1 *(to audience)*
I believe I have the right to be extremely miffed!

MASTER
Was it for me to carry for you, or was it a gift?

DISCIPLE 1
Gift, of course, but then I hoped that you could… have… re-used it?

MASTER
How *dare* you ask me for it?

DISCIPLE 1
I just feel you have refused it.

MASTER
Did you give to please me or to fill yourself with pride?
When you give to me, please leave your vanity aside.
I have money – yet more fancy shawls I can afford.
If you desire I'll have one packaged up as your reward.
But if you did this for *me*, then for my sake hold your tongue.

DISCIPLE 1
Master, please forgive me, now my pride is rightly stung.

MASTER
When you give me something, in its use you have no say.
My use for it can only be according to God's Way.
Trust in me! You do not have the gift of inner sight.

DISCIPLE 1 *(to audience)*
I'm such an idiot, of course the Master's always right.

(Exit Disciple 1.)

ACT 1, SCENE 5

(At the ashram.)

(Enter Disciple 2.)

DISCIPLE 2
Master, I took your advice regarding family duty.
Now I may immerse myself in God's immortal Beauty.
I spend more time in quiet prayer and serious reflection,
But my three sons fail to understand my new direction.
    (to audience:)
I'm listening intently for the sound of God's Command,

Then the phone rings with one more ridiculous demand.
A cricket bat, some idli chaat, please pick me up from soccer.
Saag paneer, some running gear, please get me an iced mocha.
   (to Master:)
Had I stayed unmarried I would not be in this mess!
If I could renounce them, I'd be able to progress.

MASTER
Child, I see your point, but you are acting like a fool.
Does every lonely widow study at her inner school?
No, she tames a dog or cat – some sorry waif or stray.
With food and milk she draws it in and urges it to stay.
If the cat should wander through the houses of her neighbours,
The widow then would scold them for undoing all her labours.
Without your boys, you think you would spend all day long in prayer?
No, you'd find some animal to take into your care.
Your boys are flesh and blood, are they not worth more than a cat?
As human beings are they not far more evolved than that?
To renounce the world completely goes against my teaching.
Instead of making progress, you are only over-reaching.
See God in your dear ones, see your spiritual Master,
Then you'll find your peace of mind will come to you much faster.
You will feel more love for them, concern and sweet affection.
Less of an attachment, more a meaningful connection.

ACT 1, SCENE 6

(At the ashram.)

(Enter Disciple 1. All meditate.)

DISCIPLE 2 *(to audience)*
Master told me I must meditate much more sincerely,
So that I may hear the Supreme's Will for me more clearly.
  (Master turns towards Disciple 2)
Meditate… meditate… Oh now he looks my way!
I must be having quite a high experience today.
Meditate… and still I notice he avoids her side!
Her consciousness must be so low, she hasn't even tried.
Maybe she is daydreaming, or maybe she's asleep.
What unaspiring company the Master and I keep!

DISCIPLE 1 *(to audience)*
Master, I am grateful that you only look her way –
When you treat me thus you keep my jealousy at bay.
Even your avoidance of me I take as your grace.
It is my good fortune just to look upon your face.

MASTER *(to Disciple 1)*
Good girl, you have shown me your true heart of gratitude.
I am proud of you for your surrendered attitude.
When I looked away you still were soulfully aware.

DISCIPLE 2 *(to audience)*
What? You must be kidding me, that really isn't fair!

(Exit Disciple 1.)

ACT 1, SCENE 7

(At the ashram.)

DISCIPLE 2
Master, when I first came to you, I was quite content.
Now it seems my life has turned into one long lament.
I thought in this place I'd see my happiness increase,
But I'm plagued by forces here – they give me no release.

MASTER
Ah yes, that's familiar, it's quite often the way.
Meditation is the key to keep them all at bay.

DISCIPLE 2 *(to audience)*
I'm cranky and I'm restless, I am jealous, insecure.
I'm hounded as by animals, ferocious and impure!
A tiger of destruction, or the malice of a snake.
It's like I'm in a nightmare when I'm actually awake.

MASTER
Meditate, good girl, or just immerse yourself in prayer.

DISCIPLE 2 *(to Master)*
But when I sit in silence, forces drag me to their lair.
Seems the inner journey just gets harder by the day.

MASTER
Me-di-ta-tion is the key to frighten them away.
Child, please listen to me, all these forces were inside
When you joined the spiritual life, they were just trying to hide.
Now you have invoked illumination from Above,
They're revealed, so please be happy, this is all God's Love.

DISCIPLE 2 *(to audience)*
How can I be *happy*? I feel utterly disgusting.
  (to Master:)
Why would God be testing me when I have been so trusting?

MASTER
God does not test, His only Wish is for you to grow stronger.
Even if he did, you'd not be happy for much longer
'Til you sit and pass the test, so thank Him for the chance.
Fight, my child, it is the only way you will advance.
You say your problems never end here, but that's not the case.
The only *chance* of ending them is right here in this place.
When dark forces are revealed, it's better to rejoice!
If they're hidden you will never even have the choice
Of facing them and fighting them, and ultimately slaying.
Please try to be happy. I suggest you start by praying.
Let these forces win and they will make of you a slave.
The race is for the swift, good girl, the fight is for the brave.
Just be happy, run the fastest, dive deeper within.
You are right now far more perfect than you've ever been.

(Exit Disciple 2.)

ACT 2, SCENE 1

(At the ashram.)

(Enter Disciple 1.)

DISCIPLE 1 *(to audience)*
Do I dare to share with him the contents of my heart?
No, I'm too ashamed… I might just quietly depart.
Or maybe I should do it… yes it would seem more polite

Than sneaking under cover of the dark and taking flight.
I'll spare the gruesome details of my vital and my mind.
They'd be too unsavoury to someone so refined.
He must have no idea what a mere mortal hides –
What a mess of ugliness right now in me abides.
  (to Master:)
Master, I have come to a most difficult decision.
I have tried and I have failed to live up to your vision.
I'm a constant victim to the dark and undivine –
Wild emotions, vital problems, evil thoughts are mine.
I'm leaving you to travel on my own a little while.
My very presence here I'm sure could damage and defile.
You have my word, it may take time, but I shall then return.
I don't want to cause you any trouble or concern.

MASTER
So you think by leaving here, you will not cause me trouble?
That things are easier beyond the safety of this bubble?
That you'll fare much better when you're free of my protection?

DISCIPLE 1
Master, you have showered me with blessings and affection,
But happiness eludes me, mine is quite a hopeless case.

MASTER
How can you reach the finish if you drop out of the race?
You must take medicine in a divine emergency!
Immediate relief you need, so act with urgency!
Pray and meditate: that is my spiritual prescription.

DISCIPLE 1
But I've tried, and now my torment goes beyond description.
God knows I've tried, and now I am exhausted from the fight.
Let me surrender to these forces, then they'll see the light.

They'll know that I am useless, and they'll leave me then alone.

MASTER
Child, your logic is absurd, your words I can't condone.
What would you first do if you were bitten by a snake?
Surely in a tearing rush an antidote you'd take!
What use would be the antidote long after you are dead?
Fight these enemies, this is no time to lose your head!
They have no compassion, they will never let you go,
In fact they get more dangerous the stronger that you grow.
Fight and I'll fight with you – you must win at any cost.
Give up when they've dealt their worst and you're forever lost.
Free yourself, I *urge* you, as they'll *never* set you free.

DISCIPLE 1
How is it so? You always know the way to rescue me.
Your compassion is my sword, my shield, my victory's crown.
I'll place them at your feet. Dark forces cannot drag me down.
From now on I'll please you, only you in your own way.
You're my home, my refuge, and from you I'll never stray.

ACT 2, SCENE 2

(Outside the ashram.)

(Enter Disciple 2.)

MASTER
Today we shall go for a hike and picnic in the woods.
The way is distant, so we'll need to take some worldly goods.
Kindly choose a bag to carry with you on the walk.
You may not change your mind once you've decided. Please don't talk

Amongst yourselves or look inside the bag 'til we arrive.

DISCIPLE 2 *(to audience)*
This one's so much lighter, it would almost be a skive.
With that I'll put my back out or I'll get a nasty blister.

DISCIPLE 1 *(to audience)*
Let me take the heaviest, so I may spare my sister.

DISCIPLE 2 *(to audience)*
What? She *wants* the heavy one? She must be going crazy.
Suits me, it's the weekend and I'm feeling pretty lazy.

(Disciple 1 takes heaviest, Disciple 2 takes lightest. All exit and re-enter.)

MASTER
To be in nature's beauty is itself a meditation!
Wonderful, here is the place, we've reached our destination.
So, my children, God has made a serious mistake.

DISCIPLE 2
Haha, really? Surely that is one thing God can't make!

DISCIPLE 1
Master, please explain it to us, I'm a bit confused.

MASTER *(to Disciple 2)*
It is very serious, I see you are amused.
   (to both:)
You know there are lions, tigers, bears in God's creation.
They eat only meat. Is this an ideal situation
When cows and goats and buffaloes eat only grass and leaves?
Why not give the same food as the other type receives?

Why not let them all eat meat, or let them all eat grass?
What's the point in putting each one in a certain class?
  (to Disciple 2:)
Still you think it's funny,
  (to Disciple 1:)
  and you cannot understand.
Can you not imagine it's exactly as God planned?
Maybe in a family one brother is not well,
While one is strong and stout. You think the mother cannot tell?
Of course, she uses all her wisdom and her kind concern
To feed each one a different type of meal in his turn.
When we eat at home, the food is nourishing but plain,
But when a special guest arrives, this would be too mundane.
Richer people have rich foods, not what a pauper eats –
Not dahl and rice, but rare exotic fruits and nuts and sweets.
God is not a communist, in case you weren't aware,
Yet when I treat you differently, you think I am unfair.
You feel jealous, guilty and sometimes you may protest.
Do not think each type of food is good, or better, best,
But one type is best for each according to one's needs.
As a mother, so the Master blessingfully feeds.

DISCIPLE 1
So inner nourishment may also come in different kinds.
Master, thank you, it is clear, you must have read our minds.
This morning we were criticising how you choose to treat us.
Please forgive us, we both know you'd never try to cheat us.

MASTER *(blesses both)*
Know that God has reasons for the ways of His creation,
And know that all I do is for your own illumination.
  (to Disciple 1:)
Now let us take refreshment, you have all the food and water.

I am very pleased with you, my kind and selfless daughter.
  (Disciple 1 empties her bag)
The bag that started heaviest is now light as a feather.

DISCIPLE 2 *(to audience)*
Hm... a dark cloud gathers, and I don't mean in the weather.

MASTER *(to Disciple 2)*
Open yours.

DISCIPLE 2 *(to audience)*
I have a sinking feeling in my heart.

(Disciple 2 looks in her bag.)

MASTER
Is this more a burden than it seemed back at the start?

DISCIPLE 2 *(to audience)*
Sand, clay, broken pots, all kinds of worthless stuff!

MASTER
Leave them in there for the way back home, you've seen enough.
Too late now, you each made your own choice before we started.
Have you learnt your lesson? Be more thoughtful and kind-hearted!

(Exeunt.)

ACT 2, SCENE 3

(At the ashram.)

(Enter Master and Disciple 1.)

DISCIPLE 1
Master, you have told me to expect from the Supreme,
Not from my life, but this is complicated it would seem.
I do have faith in Him, but He is not before my eyes.

MASTER
Child, some things you don't expect – they come as a surprise.
Others you expect, but then your wishes are not granted.
Then you think it's personal and you feel disenchanted.
When you set yourself a goal, do you always achieve it?
No, but this can also be God's Grace, you must believe it.
Sometimes when we use our will, we choose a lesser goal.
But this may not fulfil the true potential of our soul.
I used to want to be a ticket checker on a train! *(laughs)*
God would not have let me with my lesser goal remain.
To be a spiritual Master was my destined occupation.
My true place is here with you, not in a railway station.
There I could not fully be of service to God's Mission.
Are you happy the Supreme did not grant my ambition?

DISCIPLE 1
Master, yes! Thank God, thank you, your point is very clear.
But what happens if I have the loftiest idea?
I have prayed to God for boundless Peace and Light and Bliss.
Surely I am right to ask? Why won't He grant me this?

MASTER
You think He's jealous of you? Or you'll take away His Height?

(laughs)
It's a noble goal indeed, but is the timing right?
P'rhaps there is not room yet for an ocean in your heart,
So He gives you just a drop of nectar as a start.
If you expect and God denies, believe it is His Love.
Meditate and you may get a message from above...
Or not, perhaps, He does not owe us any explanation.
Ultimately I advise: steer clear of expectation.
Leave all to God – don't send Him any wishes to fulfil,
But peacefully, devotedly, surrender to His Will.

(Exit Disciples.)

ACT 2, SCENE 4

(At the ashram.)

(Enter Disciple 1 and Disciple 2, quarrelling.)

MASTER
Now what is the matter? Must you always fight and quarrel?

DISCIPLE 1
Master, will you help us?

DISCIPLE 2
What she says is just immoral!

MASTER
If you speak at once, how can I understand the reason?

DISCIPLE 2
Master it's outrageous, what she claims is surely treason!

Or blasphemy at least, it is too terrible to mention!

DISCIPLE 1
Master, it is you who is the bone of our contention!
The Guru's more important in my eyes than the Supreme,
As without him, we cannot fulfil God's Cosmic Dream.
The Guru takes us up to God – it's he who knows the way.
Without him, in the mire of ignorance we'd have to stay.
God cares for everyone, it's true, but if we need concern,
Or blessings in emergency, it is to you we turn.

DISCIPLE 2
I say no, this kind of love has come from the Supreme.
The Master merely plays the game, though he is on God's Team.
He's an instrument, but God has unlimited power.
The Master is the fragrance, but the Supreme is the flower.
God's the sun, and you reflect His Light, just like the moon.

DISCIPLE 1
But how will you attain that Light without the Master's boon?
How will you reach the Golden Shore unless you have a boat?
In the storms without a captain, will you stay afloat?
Then there is the question of efficient navigation!

DISCIPLE 2
Master, do you understand the source of my frustration?
The Guru came from God, and back to God he will return.
His life is temporary – maybe just so his concern.
Master, I have faith in you, but for me God is higher.

MASTER
So you wonder who will care for you when I retire?
If you take the Guru as the body, you are right.

The physical is nothing when compared to inner height.
Take the Master as the soul, then he and God are one,
But take him as the Transcendental Self, then like the sun
He's the very source of Light and not a mere reflection.
The Supreme *is* the Guru – He's the key to your perfection.
But you'll never realise God by means of separation.
Serve the Master physic'ly – this is your preparation,
Then to travel higher you must love the Master's soul.
Adore his Transcendental Self, and you will reach the goal.
Firstly, in the physical please see my boundless light,
Secondly, please feel your oneness with my own soul's height,
Then feel in this immortal Self eternal Liberation.
God and Guru are as one in the Supreme's creation –
They are *equally* important in the Cosmic Game,
As they're separated not in form, but just by name.
Ah, now my philosophy is getting far too deep!
Ah, from where to where? Now dear ones, go and get some sleep!

(Disciples bow, leave to opposite sides of the stage and go to sleep.)

ACT 2, SCENE 5

(At the ashram.)

MASTER *(to audience)*
Once these two were friends, now all they ever do is fight.
How it pains me that I cannot help them see the light.
P'raps they'll listen if I visit each one in a dream.

(Disciple 1 awakes.)

(to Disciple 1:)
Child, your quarrelling must stop, it has become extreme.
How can you be happy when you cannot get along?

DISCIPLE 1
Master, I am miserable, I don't know what went wrong!

MASTER
If you are sincere then I will give you my suggestion.

DISCIPLE 1
Tell me, please, I promise to obey you without question!

MASTER
You'll be happy only if your friend is happy too.
Tomorrow when you meet, the very first thing you must do
Is offer her your fond embrace, and at that very time
Heaven will descend on her with all its wealth sublime.
All your bitter feelings this will instantly destroy,
As you'll find true happiness in oneness with her joy.

DISCIPLE 1 *(to audience)*
Hm… this is more challenging than I would have preferred…
I'll find it in my heart to do it, as I gave my word.
We were friends, I'm sure we can become friends once again.
She might share her riches, and we'll both be wealthy then.

(Disciple 1 goes back to sleep. Disciple 2 awakes.)

MASTER *(to Disciple 2)*
Child, how can you find true joy when all you do is fight?

DISCIPLE 2
I know, but I can't help it, Master, don't you see I'm right?

I can't be happy while she lives, I absolutely *hate* her!
When she walks into the room I want to suffocate her!

MASTER
Well... that's clear... though I was hoping for a better way.
If there's no alternative let's act without delay.
Tomorrow when you leave the house and you first see her face,
Exercise great self-control and give her your embrace.
The moment that you touch her she'll immediately die.

(Exit Master.)

DISCIPLE 2 *(to audience)*
I can't *wait* for morning, that is no word of a lie.

(Leaves the house, walks towards Disciple 1.)

(to audience:)
Hold on, we were friends once, is this really the right thing?
Is it even worth it – how much karma will it bring?

(Disciple 1 awakes and leaves the house, walking towards Disciple 2, then runs to embrace her. Disciple 2 does not return the embrace.)

(to Disciple 1:)
All the wealth of Heaven has descended on me! How?
I came to embrace *you*, and you've messed it all up now!
I wanted to be happy not in *your* way, but in *mine*!
Then you stole my thunder, why must you *always* outshine?

(Enter Master.)

MASTER *(to Disciple 2)*
Fool! You would have killed her? Such a true and trusted

friend?
The cruel streak in human nature, will it never end?
She was ready to be happy only in your joy.
You were ready to dispose of her like some old toy.
See between the two of you who is by far inferior?
I want you to be as one – the lesser and superior.
Then and only then will my own mission be fulfilled.
Come, my dearest children, now your friendship please rebuild.
(to Disciple 2:)
All the inner wealth of Heaven you have now received.
Give her half, and all our dreams of joy will be achieved.
(to audience:)
My God, spiritual guidance is relentless, heavy work.
But my multifarious duties I will *never* shirk.

NOTES

1 Sri Chinmoy, *Great Indian meals: divinely delicious and supremely nourishing, part 2*, Agni Press, 1979
2 Sri Chinmoy, *Amusement I enjoy, enlightenment I study, part 3*, Agni Press, 1997
3 Sri Chinmoy, *Great Indian meals: divinely delicious and supremely nourishing, part 6*, Agni Press, 1979
4 Sri Chinmoy, *The sage Bhrigu tests the cosmic gods*, Agni Press, 2002
5 Sri Chinmoy, *Amusement I enjoy, enlightenment I study, part 5*, Agni Press, 1998
6 Sri Chinmoy, *The sage Bhrigu tests the cosmic gods*, Agni Press, 2002
7 John Bunyan, *A Pilgrim's Progress*, 1684
8 Sri Chinmoy, *Whatever you want, God gives*, Agni Press, 1994
9, 10, 11, 12, 13, 14, 15, 16 Sri Chinmoy, *The Moghul Emperors*, Agni Press, 2001
17 Sri Chinmoy, *The oneness of the Eastern heart and the Western mind*, part 3, Agni Press, 2004
18 Sri Chinmoy, *Great Indian meals: divinely delicious and supremely nourishing, part 8*, Agni Press, 1979
19 Sri Chinmoy, *The Singer of the Eternal Beyond*, Agni Press, 1973
20 Sri Chinmoy, *Great Indian meals: divinely delicious and supremely nourishing, part 8*, Agni Press, 1979
21 Sri Chinmoy, *The sailor and the parrot*, Agni Press, 1981
22 Sri Chinmoy, *The heart of a holy man*, Agni Press, 1973
23 Sri Chinmoy, *AUM — Vol. 7, No. 7, Feb. 27, 1972*, AUM Centre Press, 1972
24 Sri Chinmoy, *Life's bleeding tears and flying smiles, part 8*, Agni Press, 2001

25 Sri Chinmoy, *Great Indian meals: divinely delicious and supremely nourishing, part 10*, Agni Press, 1982
26 Sri Chinmoy, *Is your mind ready to cry? Is your heart ready to smile? part 5*, Agni Press, 1981
27 Sri Chinmoy, *Love realised, surrender fulfilled, oneness manifested*, Agni Press, 1971
28 Sri Chinmoy, *Great Indian meals: divinely delicious and supremely nourishing, part 2*, Agni Press, 1979
29 Sri Chinmoy, *Mother, give me the Light of Knowledge*, Agni Press, 1973
30 Sri Chinmoy, *Great Indian meals: divinely delicious and supremely nourishing, part 9*, Agni Press, 1979
31 Sri Chinmoy, *Great Indian meals: divinely delicious and supremely nourishing, part 2*, Agni Press, 1979
32 Sri Chinmoy, *Amusement I enjoy, enlightenment I study, part 8*, Agni Press, 1999
33 Sri Chinmoy, *Great Indian meals: divinely delicious and supremely nourishing, part 2*, Agni Press, 1979
34 Sri Chinmoy, *Great Indian meals: divinely delicious and supremely nourishing, part 3*, Agni Press, 1979
35 Sri Chinmoy, *God's new Philosophy*, Agni Press, 1974
36 Sri Chinmoy, *Great Indian meals: divinely delicious and supremely nourishing, part 2*, Agni Press, 1979
37 Sri Chinmoy, *Is your mind ready to cry? Is your heart ready to smile? part 6*, Agni Press, 1981
38 Sri Chinmoy, *Love realised, surrender fulfilled, oneness manifested*, Agni Press, 1971
39 Sri Chinmoy, *Is your mind ready to cry? Is your heart ready to smile? part 7*, Agni Press, 1981

ABOUT THE AUTHOR

Sumangali Morhall joined the Sri Chinmoy Centre in 1997, and studied meditation with Sri Chinmoy until his passing in 2007. She is a member of the Centre in York, UK, where she regularly offers free meditation courses to the public.

PREVIOUS BOOK
Auspicious Good Fortune, Mantra Books, 2012

FURTHER INFORMATION
www.sumangali.org

www.ingramcontent.com/pod-product-compliance
Lightning Source LLC
Chambersburg PA
CBHW021105080526
44587CB00010B/386